Parables of Parenthood

Parables of Parenthood

Interpreting the Gospels with Family

Andrew Taylor-Troutman

Foreword by
Brian K. Blount

Afterword by
Ginny Taylor-Troutman

RESOURCE *Publications* · Eugene, Oregon

PARABLES OF PARENTHOOD
Interpreting the Gospels with Family

All scripture references reflect the author's own work or the New Revised Standard Version unless otherwise noted.

Resource Publications
An Imprint of Wipf and Stock Publishers
199 W. 8th Ave., Suite 3
Eugene, OR 97401

www.wipfandstock.com

ISBN 13: 978-1-62564-487-9

Manufactured in the U.S.A.

Dedicated to Craig Troutman
Pastor, preacher, father, and Papi

Contents

Foreword

"I LOVE TO TELL the story . . ."

Growing up in a small Virginia town, in a small Baptist church, in a home with parents who had been deeply nurtured in the Christian faith, I came to love "the story." The Jesus story. In Sunday School, it was taught. In worship, it was preached. In wondrous music, it was sung. Even now, if I close my eyes, take a deep breath, and focus on the past, I can see and hear the Hill Street Baptist church choir singing "I love to tell the story . . ."

How I loved to hear it.

Like the Sunday school teachers whom I cherished, the pastor I appreciated, and the choir I treasured, Andrew Taylor-Troutman loves to tell the Jesus story. He has a gift for doing so. His telling of the Jesus story captivates his readers because he weaves it so seamlessly into his own human and family story. There are scholars who can exegete the biblical narratives that contain the Jesus story. And there are writers who can capture that exegesis with imaginative insight and weave it skillfully into conversation with contemporary circumstance, so that, in the end, we twenty-first century readers have the odd but comforting sense that those ancient biblical texts are talking about us.

In this book, Andrew practices both scholarship and creative writing; he has combined instructive exegesis with delightful imagination.

When I read Andrew's first book, *Take My Hand: A Theological Memoir*, and later heard him read from it and talk about it, I knew I was in the presence of someone who understands story and knows how to convey story so that it teaches and fascinates simultaneously. Connecting images from his life as a minister serving a small, rural congregation with interpretations of biblical texts and theological insight, he offered his readers a narrative portrait of what it means to be called into the deeply personal service of ministry to God's people.

It was only a matter of time before Andrew's love for the human, church, and family story and his love for biblical narrative collided so creatively in this wonderful publication.

As his work in this book amply shows, Andrew is an excellent interpreter of the New Testament parables. Operating from the original Greek, he reads the texts closely and helps readers understand the parables in their first-century context. Using the tools of biblical exegesis expertly, he compares the various versions of the parables in the three synoptic gospels, helps us understand why Mark, Matthew, and Luke offered sometimes subtle and sometimes quite distinct presentations of the same parable stories, and sharpens our focus on text details even as he helps us read those details in light of the overall objectives of the larger gospel story. In the end, we not only understand better why Mark, the first gospel, recounted one of Jesus' parables the way that it does, but we understand better why Mark's recounting is different from Matthew's or Luke's, and we understand why that difference is important.

Andrew, though, loves to tell a story. He therefore cannot help himself. While a particular parable is at the heart of each chapter, he directs us to that parable through the lens of family narration. We learn a great deal about Andrew's family as Andrew teaches us about the parables. The parables come alive because Andrew reads them as a part of what it means to be family. His adventures with his wife, Ginny, and especially his son, Sam, become the human story that surrounds and informs his reading of the Jesus story.

There were moments when reading this book that I laughed out loud, suspecting that once Andrew had extricated himself from an awkward situation he recounts, he had laughed heartily himself. There were moments when reading this book that I paused to reflect about the importance of family and how recognizing that importance can add definition to and proper respect for the priorities we set in our lives. There were moments when reading this book that, because Andrew was telling so clearly the story of engagement with his newborn son, that I was catapulted back in time to similar moments when my wife and I welcomed our newborn son into the world. But the moments I treasured the most were those carefully thought out places where Andrew brought his life with Ginny and Sam into instructive, delightful, often comical collision with Jesus' teachings about what it means to be a family, a community, a disciple, and a person.

When you have finished reading Andrew's telling of the Jesus story in relationship with his own family story, I predict you will not only have a better appreciation of some of the New Testament parables, but that you will have a better appreciation for why Jesus chose to teach in this story-like format in the first place.

Everybody loves a good story. Not everyone can tell a good story. Andrew Taylor-Troutman can.

Brian K. Blount
Richmond, Virginia
November, 2013

Acknowledgments

THIS BOOK IS DEDICATED to my dad who is my role model in both preaching and parenting. Dad and I have a love of baseball in common as well, which one day we hope to share with Sam. I think writing is like baseball in that, while each individual batter has the responsibility to hit a pitch, the game itself is the result of the coordinated efforts of many. In line with this analogy, Brian Blount is the best coach I've ever had. A terrific writer in his own right, Brian has a rare gift to coax someone else's voice instead of substituting his own. I also wish to thank my home crowd, the congregation of New Dublin Presbyterian Church, for their support and interest in this writing project and, more importantly, their love and commitment to my family. Speaking of which, special thanks to all the members of my extended family; in particular, I want to acknowledge my mom and my brother who greatly influence my thinking in uniquely wonderful ways. And I am more grateful for my wife with each passing day. Thank you, Ginny, for contributing to this book in so many countless ways. My love, we are teammates for life.

There will come a day when our son can read this book for himself. I pray that our love for him shines around each word like the morning frost on each blade of grass.

Introduction

Otherwise known as my hermeneutical approach

One of my all-time favorite snapshots was taken a few hours after my son's birth. I am sitting on a hospital sofa, the lines of exhaustion clearly visible on my face, as I smile down at this swaddled bundle held in my hands. These are first-time father's hands: awkward, anxious, yet deeply attuned. This little one in his knit cap is clearly a wonder to me. My son, Sam, holds his eyes wide open in fierce attentiveness. His brow is furrowed, as if deep in thought. Clearly, I am a marvel to him as well.

In the Gospels of the New Testament, we find snapshots of the teachings of Jesus. As I re-live my first moments with my son in some small way by looking at that favorite picture, we re-consider the kingdom of God each time we encounter an image or story from the Bible. In academic disciplines, this is called the hermeneutical approach, meaning one's method of interpretation. We study an ancient text in order to learn as much detail as possible about this snapshot and, in turn, about ourselves as interpreters. We allow our reading to speak to our hearts and minds. We offer an interpretation, not only about what we see, but also what we think; not only about what we read, but also what we feel.

This combination of head and heart knowledge is goal of this book; so before we begin, I'd like to briefly explain the theories of interpretation behind *Parables of Parenthood.*

What is a parable?

As evident in the title, the following chapters consider specific snapshots of scripture called *parables*. A "parable" is a compound word made up of a Greek preposition (*para*) that means "beside" and a Greek verb (*bole*) that means "to throw."[1] Literally the term refers to something that is thrown beside or alongside something else. This basic insight is helpful because it implies an intentional comparison between two or more objects, people, or realities. But I don't believe Jesus intended to toss things together haphazardly. So then, we must elaborate upon our basic definition by asking, what does a parable *do*? In other words, how does it affect the reader or listener?

I believe a parable is like a snapshot with a story. The best storytellers encourage their listeners to make connections and allusions, thereby allowing different people to make a version of someone else's experience a part of their own. The genius of Jesus was the ability to communicate the universe-altering concept of God breaking into this world in such a way that allows us to picture ourselves as a part of the Good News of the kingdom of heaven. In my opinion, this is "what" a parable does; more specifically, a parable *invites* the opportunity to reflect deeply upon a specific aspect of one's life alongside other experiences, even in comparison with customs or situations in the distant past.

1. Danker, *A Greek-English Lexicon*, 759–760

As Brian Blount noted in the foreword, I love to tell the Jesus story and believe that his parables offer such an amazing invitation. But the distance in time and space between us and first-century Palestine prompts other questions of interpretation. We, too, want to avoid throwing our experience haphazardly alongside the biblical text. Therefore we need to use trusted tools and methods of scholarship.

What is redaction criticism?

A hundred years or so ago, scholars thought the New Testament came into existence more or less like this: Jesus walked around, preaching and teaching in Aramaic; he died without writing anything down; for years, stories about what he did and said were circulated by word of mouth; eventually people realized they needed to record this information because the eyewitnesses to the events were almost all dead. Enter Mark, Matthew, and Luke onto the stage of history. We know little about their lives except their holy vocation. Collectively, they are responsible for the first three books of the New Testament which bear their names.

My hermeneutical approach or method of interpretation begins with this brief summary. The working assumption is that each parable first came from the historical person known as Jesus and then existed for years exclusively in the mouths and memories of people who re-told his words. However, previous theories concerning the creation of the Gospels did not paint a very flattering picture of Mark, Matthew, or Luke. They were considered to be recorders or scribes, merely copying oral tradition or other written accounts that were circulating in their time.

But then, scholars began to question this premise. What if Mark, Matthew, and Luke were smarter than we had originally thought? What if they were skilled theologians?

What if they put some thought into the way they arranged and ordered the received traditions about Jesus? And what if the stories and teachings they placed before and after each parable had something to do with their own experience? These questions sparked the creation of a method of interpretation known as redaction criticism.

Redaction criticism is most easily understood by getting inside the head of an editor at a modern newspaper. After receiving articles or reports from a variety of sources, she will double-check the grammar and correct any mistakes. Perhaps a sentence or two could be re-worded. She may also change a few phrases to strengthen or challenge other sections of the same newspaper. This last example suggests that, in addition to minute details, editors consider the larger scope of the publication because the sequence of individual stories affects the reader's interpretation of the whole newspaper. Certain reports make the front page and others are buried on the last page with the advertisements. Other articles are grouped together around a similar theme. Redaction criticism, then, involves zooming in on particular word choices in a specific parable and then panning back out to consider the overall narrative framework of the Gospel.

This analogy to a newspaper editor also implies that we need to consider the sources that the editors of the Gospels had at their disposal.

What is the Marcan Priority?

The majority of today's scholars cite a theory known as the Marcan Priority. This obtuse phrase refers to the simple idea that the Gospel of Mark was written *before* the other Gospels. The inference, then, is that Matthew and Luke used Mark's version as a reference while compiling their Gospels. While this can't be definitively proven without a time machine, I'll cite the rationale that I find to be most convincing: humans being human, our stories tend to *grow* over time. Over the course of conversation about a particular event, it is inevitable that details are added and arguments are elaborated. You would also expect the story to become increasingly polished the more often it had been told.

This relates specifically to redaction criticism because, first of all, Mark is the shortest Gospel. Secondly, Matthew and Luke follow the basic outline of Mark's sequence of material, meaning they built upon his narrative plot.[2] As we'll discover, they also refined the language of certain parables. The other two Gospels are more elegant and clear, which suggests they were editing Mark's Greek. If you imagine Mark as a mannequin, Matthew and Luke have accessorized the original arrangement.

With that metaphor in mind, let's raise a related point about another source.

What is the Q source?

There are parables shared by Matthew and Luke which are entirely absent from Mark. This provides a kind of reverse argument for the Marcan Priority. It is highly unlikely that, if Mark knew about a poignant teaching such as the Parable of the Lost Sheep, he would have deleted it from his Gospel. The logical conclusion, then, is that Matthew and Luke

2. This theory is well-evinced in modern scholarship. For an accessible summary, see Ehrman, *The New Testament*, 83–90 (especially 85–86).

shared yet another source in common that was likewise unavailable to Mark.

This concept is known as the Q Source, referring to a theoretical document identified by an abbreviation of the German word, *quelle*, which literally means "source." To be clear, no archeologist has ever discovered such a manuscript.[3] Unlike the Gospel of Mark, the existence of this document is just a theory; yet it persuasively explains how the same material, specifically numerous sayings attributed to Jesus, can be found almost word-for-word in both Matthew and Luke.

Scholars can get into heated debates about the specific content hypothesized to be found in the Q source. For my purposes, it is enough to agree with Bart Ehrman that the Q source consists of material shared by Matthew and Luke that is not in Mark.[4] To return to my metaphor, Q represents a separate clothing bin from which Matthew and Luke could rummage from and find similar items to accessorize their Marcan mannequins.

If these theories are clear, I will now explain the specifics of my head and heart approach to interpretation.

The overall structure of this book and each chapter

Here is how the method of redaction criticism is used in *Parables of Parenthood*. The book is arranged according to the chronological order of parables in Mark with additional parables following Matthew's sequence. Lessons and insights thereby build upon each other, which I believe was the intention of the Gospel editors.

3. This lack of direct evidence, however, has not prevented some scholars from building their entire *careers* on this principle, so I feel quite justified in proceeding with this little book!

4. Ehrman, *The New Testament*, 86–89

Each chapter concentrates on one parable, but compares versions in different Gospels. After a brief introduction, I have included my own translations of the Greek texts. My basic intention is to provide a convenient means to study them side-by-side. But I would also assert that every translation is itself an act of interpretation. Many English versions of the Bible smooth out the ancient languages for modern ears; I have chosen to translate the original Greek quite literally. Like a child's paint-by-numbers book, a lack of sophistication can result in greater clarity. While some of the phrases in my translations are admittedly awkward, my goal is to allow the reader to observe the Gospels as easily as distinguishing between colors.

Spring-boarding from these translations, we begin with close attention to the exact words used in Mark's parable and where it falls in relation to the larger narrative of that Gospel because this text was recorded first. Next, we study the versions of Matthew and Luke through comparison and contrast, noticing particular details that were either maintained or changed by these editors. Then, we once again expand our study in reference to the surrounding material so that we gain an appreciation of the parable functioning in the larger scope of these narratives as well. If the parable is not found in Mark, then we assume it was part of the Q source and notice the similarities and variances between Matthew and Luke. We try and think like editors through the process of zooming in on the parable and panning out to the rest of the Gospel.

Underlying this method of interpretation is my belief that the editors of the Gospels were brilliant *theologians*. They were more like composers, masterfully directing the individual parts of an orchestra (sources of information about Jesus) to achieve the best overall sound (theology about the kingdom of heaven). In the following chapters, we will discover how the music delights, soothes, and challenges our opinions and worldviews.

Finally, I would re-emphasize my earlier point about a parable as a snapshot with a story. After careful attention to the parable itself, I hope to model one way of reading the Bible through the experiential lens of modern life. Each chapter concludes with illustrations of certain insights drawn from the biblical text through my experience as a parent. These "Alongside My Son" sections are not arranged according to the chronological order of Sam's life, but spring from my reflections on the Bible. My friend, Tom, helpfully suggested coining a new term for this approach–the "hermeneutics of parenthood." I agree that it has a nice ring! More importantly, he suggests that I am reading the text and my life simultaneously, a mixture of "in print" and "in person." I think observing this dynamic will be clearer than talking about it, so I'd like to end the introduction on this note:

On October 25th, 2012 at 12:52 pm in southwestern Virginia, a newborn's high-pitched wail pierced the tension of a hospital room with a triumphant crescendo. Our midwife, Mattie, placed a wet, gooey, and healthy baby on my wife's chest. Samuel Greene Taylor-Troutman was here.

"Sam," I gasped from the side of the hospital bed, tears of joy fresh on my flushed cheeks, "I'm your dad! I'm your dad! Sam, I'm *your* dad!"

Then, he stopped crying and looked directly at me.

I met his gaze with a look of love and whispered to my wife, "Here we go."

A Velcro Swaddle

The Parable of New and Old

During those first few months of his life whenever someone asked about Sam, the subject of his sleeping habits inevitably came up, and this person would invariably have some advice. Well-intentioned people would flat out contradict each other and cite specific research to back up their divergent claims. Do you soothe your baby when he wakes up or do you let him cry until he wears himself out? Do you start your baby on solid foods before he goes to bed or continue to nurse him? Do you let your baby sleep in the bed with you or put him down exclusively in the nursery?

Over the course of navigating this maze of advice, we developed a few tricks of the trade. Ginny figured out that Sam was waking himself up because of his startle reflex, meaning that his arms would involuntarily flail around like helicopter blades at the slightest provocation. When he was about two months, we bought a special swaddle with Velcro straps. Even our little whirlwind had a hard time getting out of that one.

As first-time parents, we became keenly aware of the contrast and continuity between new and traditional parenting advice. Swaddling babies is as old as the birth of Jesus (Luke 2:7). Velcro is obviously a relatively new invention. Through trial and error, we moved forward, often discovering some kind of balance between the two.

But I have another reason for raising this specific illustration about the swaddle as the introduction to this chapter: either tradition or innovation can be *imposed* onto people. Babies have no choice. But what about adults who feel as though they are straight-jacketed by tradition or, conversely, forced to accept a new way of doing things? As a community of faith, how do we maintain the legacy that we have inherited while assuring the church remains vibrant and relevant in an ever-changing culture? These questions keep many Christians awake at night! As a result, there are contradictory and competing theories about tradition and innovation, often with each side claiming to offer the best model for today's church. To help navigate this maze of advice, let's consider what Jesus had to say about clothes and wineskins.

The Parable

Mark 2:21–22	Matthew 9:16–17	Luke 5:36–39
"No one sews a piece of unshrunk cloth onto an old garment; otherwise, the patch pulls away from it–the new from the old–and a tear becomes worse. And no one puts new wine into old wineskins; otherwise, the wine will burst the wineskins and	"No one sews a piece of unbleached cloth onto an old garment; for the patch pulls away from the garment and a tear becomes worse. And no one puts new wine into old wineskins; otherwise, the wineskins are broken apart and the	He also told them a parable: "After tearing off a piece from a new garment, no one puts it on an old garment; otherwise, it will tear the new and the piece which was from the new will not match the old. And no one puts new wine

ruin the wine and wineskins; instead new wine into new wineskins!	wine is poured out and the wineskins are ruined; instead they put new wine into new wine-skins, and both are preserved."	into old wineskins; otherwise, the new wine will burst the wineskins and it will be poured out and the wineskins will be ruined; instead new wine must be put into new wineskins. And after drinking old wine, no one wants new, for he says, 'The old is good.'"

Mark

Following the premise that Mark's Gospel was written first and referred to by Matthew and Luke, let's begin by examining a few literary features of this book of the Bible. Scholars have long noticed that Jesus hits the ground running in Mark's Gospel. One of the evangelist's favorite words is "immediately," which he uses to narrate Jesus' movements and actions in rapid fire sequence. As a reader, I barely have time to catch my breath until, *boom*, Jesus is doing something different again! Some interpreters have understood this tendency as evidence that Mark was a sloppy story-teller or that he was juvenile, flailing out facts like a newborn's startle reflex. But such conclusions miss the rhetorical point of his style.

While Mark narrates this good news in a breathless, almost frantic pace, his Gospel is not unsophisticated. It is composed like a series of front page headlines: "Extra, extra! Read all about it!" Jesus begins his ministry by announcing that the time has been fulfilled and the kingdom of God has come near (Mark 1:14–15). From Mark 1:21 through 2:12, the healings and exorcisms that he performs witness to the power that God has unleashed on the world–boom! In Jesus, God is doing something fantastic, something *new*. This is especially relevant because our parable is prompted by a question about the traditional practice of fasting.

The in-breaking of God's kingdom in the person of Jesus Christ affects everything in the world, including religious rituals and practices. As Pheme Perkins puts it, "Conventional rules do not apply."[1] In the Old Testament, the practice of fasting has a rich history as an example of both communal and personal devotion to God. The Law required fasting only on the Day of Atonement (Lev 16:1–34; 23:26–32; Num 29:7–11); however, there were other fast days added later in history (Ezra 8:21–23; Neh 9:1; Zech 8:19). We also find record of impromptu fasts observed by large numbers of people because of a national emergency (Esth 4:16; Isa 58:3–6; Jonah 3:5). Other texts record fasts as personal expressions of supplication, mourning, repentance (1 Sam 1:7–8; Neh 1:4; Dan 9:3). Therefore it makes sense that the disciples of the Pharisees and of John the Baptist observe fasts and question Jesus about the seeming negligence of his disciples (Mark 2:18). Why aren't they likewise following this important and sacred tradition?

Jesus responds to this question with figurative language, which might catch modern readers off-guard. His interlocutors asked about fasting; why is he discussing wedding banquets? The key is that we understand the symbolism. By the time of Jesus, the coming of God's kingdom in the new age was imagined as a great banquet or wedding feast.[2] The "new" aspect to Mark's theology is that this reality has *already begun* in the person of Jesus the Messiah.

1. Perkins, "The Gospel of Mark," 554
2. Boring, "The Gospel of Matthew," 235

Accordingly, Perkins believes that the wedding banquet image "symbolizes the presence of salvation."[3] What's more, "The fasting episode signifies that, because they are with Jesus, the disciples act as though the kingdom of God is present."[4]

In Mark, Jesus' response to the question of fasting does not imply a critique of the spiritual discipline, but rather of the specific *timing*. This interpretation implies a sharp rebuke: if guests are fasting during the wedding, then they are *disapproving* of the marriage and *insulting* the host.[5] The Pharisees and John's disciples were correct in noting the differences between their communities and the one forming around Jesus; according to Mark, however, they are the ones who are at fault, even though they believe they are following a traditional practice of devotion to God.

Mark employs the parables about new cloth and new wine to play on this irony. An "old garment" is ruined by the patch, not repaired. The contrast between "new and old" pieces of clothing is explicit (Mark 2:21). Likewise new wine "bursts" and destroys old wineskins because the new wine ferments and gives off gases that break the brittle fabric of the containers (Mark 2:22).

In his explosive style of writing, Mark uses these parables to lay down the *boom*! Even cherished expressions of piety and traditional religious practices must be questioned in light of the reality of God's reign in the person of Jesus Christ. The old guard is more than put off-guard by this new, bombastic understanding: they are threatened. Within the first three chapters of this Gospel, the religious leaders move from questioning Jesus about the habits of his

3. Perkins, 555
4. Perkins, 557
5. Perkins, 555

disciples to conspiring with their political officials in order to kill him (Mark 3:6). Extra, extra! Read all about it!

Luke

Luke's version shares many similarities with Mark's account. Both Gospels narrate the same events in roughly the same sequence that lead up to Jesus' statements about the new and old: the call of the first disciples (Mark 1:16; Luke 5:1), the cleansing of a leper (Mark 1:40; Luke 5:12), the healing of a paralytic (Mark 2:1; Luke 5:17), and the call of Levi (Mark 2:13; Luke 5:27). By building on the narrative framework in Mark, Luke ratchets up the contrast between old and new.

In Luke, the hypothetical situation involves first tearing up a new garment in order to produce a patch for an old one. This idea is obviously ridiculous: surely no one would do such a thing (Luke 5:36). In addition, the language that Mark used to describe the patch of cloth as "unshrunk" or unwashed is replaced by the notion that the old clothing does not "match" or compliment the new (Mark 2:21; Luke 5:36). According to Luke, the two types of cloth have a fundamental difference that cannot be changed or fixed. Furthermore Luke emphasizes that the new wine "*must* be put" it new wineskins (Luke 5:38; emphasis mine). The effect of these subtle changes to Mark's version makes even sharper distinctions: apparently Luke is not at all interested in patching up the old garment or preserving the old wineskins. Alan Culpepper states emphatically that, in this version of the parable, Luke allows "no accommodation between the old and the new. The new will supersede and displace the old."[6]

6. Culpepper, "The Gospel of Luke," 131

Culpepper also points to the significance of a verse that is completely unique to Luke: "And after drinking old wine, no one wants new, for he says, 'The old is good'" (Luke 5:39). This statement may seem as innocuous as a glass of red wine with dinner, but Culpepper insists, "[This is] one of the Gospel's most piercing judgments. As Christians in a privileged society, have we cultivated such a taste for the old wine that we despise the new?"[7] In other words, have we become too comfortable with our traditions? Have we developed such a preference for the finer, more expensive things in life that we are missing out on the dramatically new thing God is doing? In Luke's hands, I am reminded of Isaiah's prophetic announcement, "Behold, I am doing a new thing! Do you not perceive it?" (Isa 43:19).

Matthew

While likewise building upon Mark's Gospel, Matthew's version serves as a counterpoint to Luke's emphasis. Like wine connoisseurs, careful readers of this Gospel will detect subtle variations in flavor. The root of such distinctions can primarily be understood by differences in their original audiences. There is consensus among scholars that the first recipients of Matthew's Gospel were primarily Jews who began following Jesus as the Messiah, while Luke wrote to a largely Gentile audience. With this hypothesis in mind, we would expect Matthew to exhibit more continuity and connection with the past than either Luke or Mark.

While Matthew preserves much of the same language, it deletes Mark's specific reference to "the new from the old" (Mark 2:21). As reflected in my translations above, the same Greek adjective may be translated as either "unshrunk" or

7. Culpepper, 132

"unbleached."[8] For Matthew, the problem was that the patch wasn't treated correctly, and so it pulls away from the garment; instead of fulfilling its purpose, it makes the rip worse (Mt 9:16). In addition, notice that Matthew slyly adds to the description of wine and wineskins that "both are preserved" (Mt 9:17). Can such slight changes to parables dramatically change their meaning? What might Matthew be trying to communicate to his original audience and to us?

In the Sermon on the Mount, Jesus famously states, "Do not think that I have come to abolish the Law or the Prophets. I have not come to abolish, but to fulfill" (Mt 5:17). In terms of the parables, the old garment does not need to be destroyed, but repaired; the new wine needs to be placed in the proper containers, so that neither are destroyed. Biblical scholar Eugene Boring might have an unfortunate name for someone who publishes, but I have always found his insights to be stimulating. He makes note of these differences and concludes, "Matthew sees Jesus as having brought something eschatologically new . . . But Jesus brings the eschatologically new in such a way that it does not do away with the old, but fulfills and preserves it."[9] The new is in continuity with the old; the new perfects tradition, instead of getting rid of it.

Conclusion

It is important that we recognize the variations in the different Gospels because they give us an insight into the original communities and the struggles they faced. Specifically I hope it was clear that the make-up of the original audience of a particular Gospel impacted how they interpreted their

8. Danker, *A Greek-English Lexicon*, 12

9. Boring, 236

community's relationship to the past. This is true today as well. Like first-time parents, the church today must carefully weigh the arguments for maintaining tradition versus implementing new ideas in a rapidly evolving culture. Occasionally we should take to heart Luke's insistence that we need to change and let go of our outdated ways in order to experience a fresh perspective. In other circumstances, we do well to hear Matthew's call to carry forward with the best of tradition, even as we seek to live into a new day. Sometimes the way forward is a form of compromise, like our experience with the Velcro swaddle, as we find a balance between the new and the old. I'd like to think about these ideas through the illustration of naming our son, Samuel Greene Taylor-Troutman.

Alongside My Son

Called by Name

When we were married, Ginny and I decided to hyphenate our last names. We wanted to start our new life together with the symbolic understanding that both families of origin are important. A hyphen creates one word from two separate ones, meaning that something new is actually the result of maintaining a direct reference to both traditions. As people learned of this decision, the most common question involved our children: Would they also have a hyphenated last name? Yes! We wanted to pass along this value of equal preservation, while starting something new with our nuclear family—the Taylor-Troutmans. Once the last name was decided, we were left the not-so-simple decision about the rest of our child's name . . .

We had made up our minds, even before she was pregnant, that we wanted to learn the sex of our baby as soon as possible. In part, this had to do with plans and preparations; but mostly we wanted to select the name in advance. I'm sure that you've probably got a great story about naming your child just after you first laid eyes on the baby . . . but we simply could not wait!

After the ultrasound proved convincingly that we were having a boy (that is a story for another chapter), we discussed this important decision over lunch at our favorite restaurant. As we ate quiche and soup, we touched on this name and that one. We wanted a name for our newborn that reflected our joy about this unique and wondrous gift, yet also reminded us of our family history. In seeking the perfect balance, there were several good options but none that seemed quite right. That is, until I suggested Samuel Greene Taylor-Troutman. I'll never forget Ginny's face, as she lit up and whispered reverently, "That's *perfect*."

In the Old Testament, a boy named Samuel was the fulfillment of Hannah's fervent prayer for a child after a long period of infertility (1 Sam 1:13–16). We, too, knew something about the agonizing uncertainty of those prayers (yet another tale for later in this book). But the child's name evokes the incredible feeling of grace when the wait is *over*. In Hebrew, "Samuel" is a play on the words, "name" and "God." Hannah thought that her son was named by God (1 Sam 1:20). But the Hebrew letters embedded in Sam's name can also form the verb, to hear, as in "God has heard." Our son is an answer to our prayers and we want to raise him in our faith tradition, which includes the story of his namesake and how this scripture is God's Living Word in our lives.

Sam's middle name, Greene, is the maiden name of my maternal grandmother. Like many family names, it has a history tied to a place and time. To this day, members of the Greene family live in Oxford, North Carolina, which is a small, agricultural town with a Baptist church that all my relatives attended. Shortly after Ginny and I began dating, the community marked its one hundred and fiftieth year with a sesquicentennial celebration. For the Greenes, it was really more like a family reunion; but the truth is that I didn't want Ginny to attend this reunion. At that time in my life, I was ashamed of this side of my family.

Timothy Tyson has written a book, *Blood Done Sign My Name*, about the horrific racism in Oxford during the Civil Rights era, including the real-life story of cold-blooded murder of a young black man.[10] My relatives lived during this sad history and one of them, my great uncle, actually appears in the book. He was the man who bought the public swimming pool in order to maintain segregation by making it private property. He couldn't even swim; but he was racist and had the money to prove it. As difficult as it is for me to imagine, he must have thought that he was maintaining a just and noble tradition. In fact, segregation blinded him to the reign of God that demanded a new way of living regardless of skin color and ethnicity. For such shameful reasons, I didn't want Ginny to even visit the place or meet these relatives. Years later, why in the world would I want to name my son after this side of the family? What about new wine and old wineskins?

Like many small churches, there is a cemetery just outside the little Baptist church in Oxford. After the sesquicentennial celebration, we stood under a big blue canopy of a sky and my dad told me about the women of the Greene family, about how they would gather around family tombstones after funerals. The older generations would share the stories about the departed, such as the one about my great-great-grandmother who allegedly chased away Union troops with a kitchen broom! While the veracity of these

10. Tyson, *Blood Done Sign My Name*

tales might not stand close scrutiny, the abiding message related to the strength of these women. And so, the new generations would hear these stories about the seemingly ancient past, no doubt embellished, but nonetheless a part of family history meant to inspire the future.

While there is racism snaking its way up my family tree, there are also strains of fierce independence that have rooted my relatives during difficult times. So it's not as simple as replacing the old with the new: I do not want my son to be blind or indifferent to the skeletons in our family closet. Yet, instead of denying the past and the reality of its mistakes, I hope that Samuel Greene will study our cultural history and learn from the best lights of his own family tradition.

A Privilege

For Mark, I have argued that it was an important aspect of his rhetorical style to write his Gospel at frantic speed. Not only does this convey the sense that the reign of God was breaking into the world, but it puts a special emphasis on the listener to hurry and convert. Extra, extra! Read all about it! Believe in the good news and repent (Mark 1:15)! But I would also note how Jesus drew on basic observations from the world of his listeners, like wineskins and clothes. Some scholars suggest these parables are more similar to a proverb or wisdom saying.[11] At first blush, these illustrations involved basic commonsense; but with contemplation, the meaning deepens profoundly. In a sense, his parables were passed on like family stories, perhaps embellished and glossed by subsequent storytellers, but for the purpose of connecting with a new listener in a different situation. The

11. Williamson, *Mark*, 69–70

key is that, when the message hit home, you could never forget what the lesson meant to you.

Ironically it seems to me that the people who plotted to *kill* Jesus understood his message in a deeper way than many Christians in our country. When Jesus spoke, they realized that he was a threat to their way of life. Like the Civil Rights era attacked white supremacy in the South, so the Good News of Jesus Christ broke down political and religious barriers designed to keep people in places of inferiority. From our position of opulence and affluence, we are often too comfortable with our ways. But, if we claim to be disciples of Jesus, then we should be trying to live like the one who continued the traditions of Israel yet simultaneously turned the world on its head. For people of privilege, this paradox means taking a critical view of cherished traditions because, too often, what has been sacred to a few has been detrimental to many. Rather than denying the past, we need to study it carefully. We need to show up at the sesquicentennial celebrations and remember the past for its cruelty and horror in order to find a redemptive story.

I love the dedication of Walter Brueggemann's book, *Prayers for a Privileged People*: "I am glad to dedicate this book to my new grandson, Peter William Brueggemann, who, like many of us, is born into some privilege and invited to a life of reflection, yielding, and glad obedience."[12] This is one of my prayers for Samuel Greene Taylor-Troutman. I pray that, for the rest of his unique and wondrous life, his name will remind him of where he comes from, both in his faith and family traditions. Not a perfect past, but not to be forgotten either: a blending of old and new like when he was wrapped so lovingly in a Velcro swaddle.

12. Brueggemann, *Prayers for a Privileged People*, v

Seeds of Grace

The Parable of the Sower

LET ME FIRST SAY that I am grateful for each person's kind support of Sam and our family. But, while thankful for every *giver*, there are a few *gifts* that I would gladly do without! If the toy makes noise, then I am inclined to bury the present in the back of Sam's closet, which serves as a kind of purgatory for all manner of musical stuffed animals and squawking electronic games.

On the other hand, certain gifts have special places of honor. His favorite books are prominently displayed in his nursery, right next to the rocking chair. And we have stacks and stacks of more books under coffee tables throughout the house, so that we can pull them out to read at a moment's notice. I am aware this might involve a certain amount of projection on my part, particularly when I insist that these are Sam's "favorite" toys. However, he genuinely loves the special ones, like the book about owls that includes pages with feathered eyebrows, shiny eyes, and sandpaper claws. He pats, pulls, and pokes these tactile images, and the only sounds emitted are his own contented coos and playful giggles.

One morning at church, a kind and thoughtful woman came to my office with the gift of a beautiful book called *Plant a Kiss.*[1] The story involves a young girl who digs a hole in the ground and literally plants a kiss. After a period of waiting in which she diligently waters and cares for the kiss, it "sprouts" into a kaleidoscopic fountain of glittery bright colors. The girl collects this "fruit" into a red bowl and shares it with other children, far and wide. When the bowl is emptied, she returns and discovers that the magic of the kiss never runs out.

Once again, I may be accused of projecting my own values, in this case onto a biblical text, but this hopeful message reminds me of the famous Parable of the Sower. This teaching is a favorite of many faithful people and perhaps the parable that we most often hear in church, especially around children. We will shortly consider the validity of the popular interpretation that urges us to be like the good soil; but I believe the fundamental teaching highlights God's fantastic grace from seemingly insignificant beginnings. So rather than consign the parable to the back of the closet by thinking we've already figured it out, let's explore the texts anew with wonder like a child.

1. Rosenthal, *Plant a Kiss*

The Parable

Mark 4:2–9	Matthew 13:3–9	Luke 8:4–8
He began teaching them in many parables and said to them in this teaching: "Listen! Behold the sower who went out in order to sow. And in the sowing, some fell beside the road, and birds came and devoured it. And other seed fell on the rocky ground where there was not much soil; and immediately, it sprang up because the soil was not deep. And when the sun rose, it was burnt and, because it did not have roots, it was dried out. And other seed fell in the thorns, and the thorns came up and choked it, and it did not give fruit. But others fell in the good soil and were giving fruit after coming up and growing and bearing thirty and sixty and one hundredfold." And he said, "Whoever has ears to hear, listen!"	And he told them many things in parables, saying: "Behold! The sower went out to sow. And as he sowed, some fell beside the road and, after they came, the birds devoured them. Others fell on the rocky ground where there was not much soil; and immediately, it sprang up because the soil was not deep. And after the sun rose, it was burnt and, because it did not have roots, it was dried out. Others fell on the thorns, and the thorns came up and choked them. But others fell on the good soil and were giving fruit, some one hundredfold, some sixty, and some thirty. Let the one who has ears, listen!"	He spoke through a parable: "The sower went out in order to sow his seed. And in his sowing, some fell beside the road and was trampled under foot, and the birds of heaven devoured it. And another fell down upon the rock and, after it grew, was dried out because it did not have moisture. And another fell in the middle of thorns, and as the thorns grew with it, they choked it. But another fell in the beneficial soil and, after it grew, produced fruit one hundredfold." After he said these things, he called out, "Let the one who has ears to hear, listen!"

Encouragement and Exhortation

Before we consider each version in the Gospels, I briefly want to offer some introductory comments because the Parable of the Sower is arguably Jesus' most well-known teaching; yet, our familiarity with this text may have more to do with each Gospel's subsequent explanation than the actual parable itself.

In Matthew, Mark, and Luke, Jesus interprets the parable as an allegory, meaning that each fictional item in the parable has a real-life, corresponding element in the world (Mt 13:18–23; Mark 4:13–20; Luke 8:11–15). The seed is the Word of God; the birds that gobble up the seed are like the Devil; the rocky ground represents temptation; the thorns that choke the young plants symbolize the effect of material possessions. The good soil represents people who "understand" the Word (Mt 13:23) or "accept it" (Mark 4:20) or "hold it fast in an honest and good heart" (Luke 8:15). Though each Gospel writer has a unique twist on the exact formulation the main teaching point, it is clear that each summary statement fulfills the same purpose in an allegorical interpretation: we are urged to become like the good soil. Of course, there is nothing wrong with this exhortation. But with the assistance of astute scholarship, we can discern other valuable meanings that may not have been previously appreciated.

Lamar Williamson recognizes two lines of interpretation: *exhortation*, which is the common view expressed above, and *encouragement*.[2] In order to discern this second motivation, we must focus on the parable itself and resist skipping ahead to the allegorical interpretation. Williamson maintains that a sense of encouragement is found in the repeated contrast between small, discouraging beginnings and great, satisfying endings. Matthew follows Mark in stating that the three examples of seed that do not produce are then immediately followed by three degrees of increasingly abundant yield–thirty, sixty, and hundredfold (Mark 4:8; Mt 13:8). What's more, the sower maintains a confident

2. Williamson, *Mark*, 88

initiative despite the waste inherent in the ancient sowing practice of broadcasting seed over a large area. Farming in this fashion takes a lot of faith! Without denying the exhortation to become like the good soil, Williamson wants to nuance this interpretation: "What the listener is exhorted to hear is good news."[3] In other words, the parable is not only about doing the right thing, but also bears a message of grace. We can trust that God interacts with the world and, despite apparent setbacks, brings about the kingdom of heaven in increasingly fantastic ways.

Using Williamson's dual emphasis of exhortation and encouragement, let's now consider each Gospel and see if we can determine how different versions emphasize one motivation over the other.

Mark

In his lucid analysis, Gary Charles notes the importance of another parable unique to Mark, often referred to as the Parable of the Growing Seed (Mark 4:26–29). This, too, is about a sower; however, the emphasis is not on human action but the soil itself, which "automatically" brings forth the plant (Mark 4:28). We derive our English word, automatic, from the Greek word that describes how the earth produces the grain. Charles concludes, "The future of God's reign will depend less on [our] efforts than on the mysterious and yet trustworthy ways of God."[4] Coming on the heels of the Parable of the Sower, this parable may well have been intended by Mark to re-frame the early teaching along the lines of encouragement by emphasizing God's "automatic"

3. Williamson, 91

4. Blount and Charles, *Preaching Mark*, 65

grace instead of the use of physical effort or mental energy by humans.

As evidence of this claim, it is fascinating to note that Mark has Jesus tell the disciples right after the Parable of the Sower that they have been given the "secret" of the kingdom of God (Mark 4:10). This word could also be translated as "mystery" but the larger point is that, in Matthew and Luke, the disciples receive the *secrets* or the *mysteries*–the plural forms of the same noun (Mt 13:11; Luke 8:10). According to Williamson, the importance of this singular versus plural usage is that, in Mark, *Jesus* is the secret whereas Matthew and Luke are talking about other details concerning the kingdom of God: "[In Mark] Jesus communicates no privileged information about the kingdom. Rather, in the authentic speaking and hearing of the parables, Jesus gives the kingdom itself."[5] The kingdom is a gift from God brought about through Jesus, not only in his teachings but also his life, death, and resurrection. This grace is encouraging news indeed.

Matthew

Reflecting upon Matthew's slight change to the singular "secret" found in Mark, one might then notice other distinctive features about other verses surrounding the parable. For example, this Gospel attributes the justification for speaking in parables to Isaiah and then expands the citation (Mt 13:13–15; Mark 4:12). Matthew alone has Jesus explicitly mention the "dull hearts" of certain people thereby re-emphasizing the contrast between those who "get it" and

5. Williamson, 92

those who do not.[6] We should suspect that such emphasis was intentional.

The adamant emphasis upon this insider/outsider theme is further highlighted by yet another parable found only in one Gospel; in this case, the Parable of the Wheat and Tares (Mt 13:24–30). Once again, we read about a sower and, in an obvious echo to the previous parable, we also hear about good seed. But now, an enemy comes secretly and sows "tares" or weeds among the wheat. Just as we found in relation to the Parable of the Sower, Matthew has Jesus explain the meaning of this second parable to his disciples in allegorical fashion: the sower is the Son of Man contrasted with the enemy who is the Devil; the wheat are the children of the kingdom in opposition to the children of evil (Mt 13:36–39). Especially in light of the final judgment, when both wheat and weeds will be gathered and the latter thrown into the fire, this is clearly a call to exhortation (Mt 13:40–43). Matthew even has Jesus repeat the exact same phrase as a concluding charge, "Let the one who has ears, listen!" (Mt 13:9; 13:43). As we would expect from a skillful editor, the close proximity of this second parable to the Parable of the Sower reinforces its primary message: be good soil . . . or else!

Luke

It would seem that Luke will break the tie between emphasis on encouragement (Mark) or exhortation (Matthew). On the other hand, this Gospel might reveal a new insight. Unlike the other Gospels, Luke prefaces the parable by mentioning certain women who were in the company of Jesus. Mary Magdalene will appear later, but neither this

6. Senior, *The Gospel of Matthew*, 124–125

Joanna nor Susanna are mentioned again (Luke 8:3). It seems unlikely that Luke was merely dropping names if these women were so unrecognizable. Perhaps, then, they provide an interpretative lens for the parable itself.

These women and other unnamed companions had been cured of "evil spirits and infirmities" and were now using their resources to take care of Jesus and the rest of the disciples (Luke 8:2–3). Literally Luke tells us the women were "ministering" to the men. Since the parable immediately follows, are we to discern that these women represent the good soil? If so, this would be quite unexpected because women were considered to be inferior to men in the ancient world (that statement will be unpacked in a later chapter). For now, note that the correlation of these women with good soil would also be surprising, even shocking, because at least one of them had a notorious reputation among Luke's community: Mary Magdalene was formerly possessed by *seven* demons (Luke 8:2).

A few verses after the Parable of the Sower, Jesus learns that his mother and siblings were requesting his presence. He responds, "My mother and my brothers are those who hear the word of God and do it" (Luke 8:21). This has been interpreted as a harsh response, even a sign of disrespect; but I believe the previous Parable of the Sower sheds light on Luke's intended meaning. The good soil is evinced, not by its prior condition, but by the *results*. As Williamson noted, "What the listener is exhorted to hear is good news."[7] Those who have been in difficult situations can take heart because they can live out their faith through ministry to others, like these women of Luke's Gospel. For Luke, receiving God's grace does entail a responsibility; but let's not forget that the gift is extended to *all* people, including those we might not expect, like notorious women. Maybe like you and me.

7. Williamson, 91

Conclusion

Williamson maintains that it is misleading for an interpreter to suggest than a parable only has one message: "As metaphorical mode of communication, parables are open to multiple meanings."[8] So let's be clear what we are *not* saying: Mark's use of the parable is only for encouragement, while Matthew exclusively exhorts his audience. What we found to be true with Luke is essentially true for the other Gospels: *both* motivations are clearly present in each. Yet I believe that it is instructive to notice how these ancient editors nuanced the message one way or the other, presumably in order to motivate their original audience. Whether as a preacher, a Sunday School teacher, or a parent, we do the same with Jesus' teachings. That does *not* mean that we can force the parables into saying whatever we want, but according to Williamson, entails a serious responsibility: "The art of the interpreter is to follow the lead of scripture by taking up these stories in ever-new situations, allowing them the freedom to speak with fresh nuances while assuring continuity with their meaning in the canonical context."[9] I would now like to offer such an example from my own experience.

Alongside My Son

Growth Stories

My greatest hope is that, despite evidence to the contrary, God is present and active in human history; in response to this divine initiative, I strive to be like the good soil in my daily life, including the relationships with my family.

8. Williamson, 89
9. Williamson, 89

And so, there are elements of both human effort and divine grace, as encouragement and exhortation are not necessarily contrasted but ideally harmonized. Apparent contradictions blur together, as parents inspire hope and offer advice, thereby imparting both confidence and admonition to their children.

Speaking in terms of my life, a typical workday ends when I walk in through the back door, feed the dog, and read books with my son until Ginny comes home from the gym. While Sam is sitting in my lap, babbling away and patting a bright illustration, I often wonder what he is learning. What seeds are being planted and what lessons will produce fruit later in his life? Will he learn to trust in God's grace, even if a situation appears hopeless? Will he keep trying, even if the results are frustrating? Will he remember that seemingly small and even insignificant actions can actually mean everything to someone in need?

These questions can lead to healthy exhortation; however, if one is not careful, the desire to nurture a child can be more like an anxious farmer stressed over his crop. When we first brought Sam home, I would get up, still half asleep, and frantically search the covers for Sam, convinced that I had left him in the bed and was smothering him. Of course, he was in the bassinet, sleeping blissfully unaware of his dad's anxiety. "False alarm," Ginny would whisper exasperatedly, as she tugged me back in bed.

I don't think of myself as a "worrywart" so much as I worry about each of Sam's warts! Ginny has to counteract my anxiety about red bumps on Sam's arms ("Those are mosquito bites, not tumors"), his excessive drool ("He's teething and does not have a hereditary disease") and that suspicious build-up in his ear ("Come on, Andrew, it's *just* ear wax!").

I also worry that Sam is going to be hurt. Sadly, some accidents really do happen. Once I pinched his skin while attempting to buckle him into a high chair. He cried out and looked up at me with tears in his eyes, as if to say, *How could you?* Another time I forgot to turn the hot water completely off while filling the bathtub. The temperature was not hot enough to pose a real danger, but enough that, when I put my son down in the water, his eyes got big and he sucked in his breath. I scooped him back up immediately, but he still wailed pitifully. Surely he doesn't remember these isolated incidents: Sam loves to eat at restaurants and take baths. Nonetheless I *still* feel guilty.

I've heard it said that the goal of a parent is not to burden the child with things he or she has to unlearn later in life. Everyone makes mistakes, but I don't want to sow ideas or attitudes in Sam's consciousness that eventually he will have to weed out. And I don't want my stress about his future to devour, wither, or suffocate his joy.

In his deeply moving and tragically beautiful memoir which chronicles his son's eventual death, Richard Lischer shares about a day when his son, Adam, came home and announced that he had earned a terrific role in the high school musical: "He was bursting with pleasure [Lischer remembers]. 'You won't believe what happened today!' Without so much as a word of congratulations, I promptly asked him if the play would interfere with his studies. I can still see his face falling. That was not a fight, but worse than a fight."[10]

At the time of this recollection, Lischer was sitting at a café with Adam who only had a few more weeks to live. I can't imagine that scene without tears coming to my eyes, but thankfully, the conversation did not end on a note of regret. Recalling that bad memory from years long ago, Adam

10. Lischer, *Stations of the Heart*, 151

smiles, "You didn't have other sons to practice on . . . I never give your mistakes a thought."

To which Lischer replies, "I've been relying on your forgiveness for years."

"You can do that," Adam says and smiles shyly.[11]

By keeping such encouragement in mind, maybe then I can become more aware of the fruit of grace. My own father once told me that every adult must first put his or her parents on trial, and then find them *guilty*. We all make mistakes and honestly coming to terms with the failures of your own parents is part of the process of becoming your own person. "Yet," my dad says with his own shy smile, "What you hope and pray is that your son pardons your crimes against him." In other words, we must hope that God's grace blossoms in abundance.

Since those first nightmares, I've learned that there are a myriad of other things to worry about as a parent. I'm quite sure that the future will reveal other fears, both real and imagined. But as Sam grows, I'm going to try and trust God, the One who creates lasting beauty from even the smallest of events.

Accordingly, I've come to think that reading to my son is analogous to sowing seed; perhaps every book will not stick with him, but I have faith that something sacred is being nurtured. Sometimes when we are reading, Sam will stop playing with the book long enough to turn around, look directly in my eyes, and smile shyly. At that moment, I know that we are sowing seeds of grace, which multiply thirty, sixty, and a hundredfold.

11. Lischer, 152

Foundation with Food

The Parable of the Two Builders

THEY TELL A CUTE story at the church I serve about a toddler who couldn't keep up with the older children during the annual Easter egg hunt. The day was almost over and this poor little guy didn't have even one plastic egg in his basket. That's when the pastor, a tall man in his sixties, crossed purposefully across the yard to where this young parishioner stood, crying pitifully, and ceremoniously presented him with an egg. The little boy then ran and told his mommy that he had received an Easter egg . . . *from God*!

From little children to adults, lay people often have assumptions about clergy–who we are and what we do–and, sometimes, we are held in very high regard. But for the record, no one has ever confused me with any deity. Even as a young child, I never made that association either because I grew up as a pastor's kid. We are very quickly disabused of the notion that the woman or man standing in the pulpit is God. We know their rough edges and how often they make mistakes.

Speaking of which, I remember one particularly long night in which Sam had been up a half dozen or so times. I was walking around our bedroom with him in my arms, bouncing him up and down, and swinging him from side to side in the futile effort to lull him to sleep. Exhausted, I was on a kind of parental autopilot. My wife, who was extremely attuned to Sam's sobs, grew impatient and, in no uncertain terms, ordered us out of the room. I countered that I was too tired and quite ready for her to take a turn with the baby. She icily reminded me that she had just spent the past hour nursing Sam and needed some rest herself. To which I responded with a few choice words about her being selfish and lazy. Now do you understand that pastors make mistakes?

Before our argument could escalate even further, Sam's diaper suddenly leaked a steady stream of pee down the front of my shirt. At that exact moment, Sam stopped crying and I swear he gave both of us a look that said, *Lighten up, will you?* Ginny and I fell into a stunned silence . . . and then simultaneously burst out laughing!

Poor Sam; he is a preacher's kid two times over. He's going to need a sense of humor! But, despite all the unenlightened, rash, and inconsiderate things we say, Ginny and I do tell him, on multiple occasions every single day, that he is *loved*. We are not perfect, much less God-like; but through all of life, we are committed to living from this foundation of love, which Jesus once symbolized as building on the rock.

The Parable

Matthew 7:24–27	Luke 6:47–49
"Therefore, all who hear these words of mine and do them will be like a wise man, who built his house on the rock. And the rain came down and rivers came and the winds blew and they beat against that house, but it did not fall for it had been established on the rock. And all who hear these words of mine and do not do them will be like a foolish man, who built his house on the sand. And the rain came down and the rivers came and the winds blew and they dashed against that house and it fell. And its fall was great."	"All who come to me and hear my words and do them, I will explain to you who that person is like–like a person building a house who dug and dug deep and put a foundation on the rock. After the flood came, the river burst upon that house, but it was not strong enough to shake it because it was built well. But the one who hears and does not do is like a person who built a house on the ground without a foundation. The river burst upon it and, immediately, it collapsed. And the ruin of that house became great."

Matthew and Luke

Both Gospels record the Parable of the Two Builders as the conclusion of a long discourse of Jesus' teaching, which is generally referred to as the Sermon on the Mount (Mt 5:1–7:27) and the Sermon on the Plain (Luke 6:20–47). But despite this over-arching similarity, a careful reader will note distinctions between Matthew's and Luke's versions. Matthew has a "wise" builder setting a house on rock and another "foolish" builder on sand, while Luke contrasts laying a foundation versus omitting one. In addition, Matthew envisions a violent storm that destroys the second home, but Luke describes a raging flood. How do we account for these dissimilarities?

Scholars have offered explanations by considering the original audience, particularly with respect to their cultural practices in response to the local environment.[1] The hypothesis that makes the most sense to me is that Matthew is describing a setting familiar to native Palestinian residents. In this part of the world during the first century, it was common practice to lay a foundation for a house on rock, but a "foolish" practice to build on sand because the latter is often the dry bed of a seasonal river. When the rainy season arrives, storms fill the riverbeds with water and often result in widespread floods, which overwhelm anything in the way, including buildings. The inference is that the second person was foolish for choosing a building site without considering the consequences. By contrast, the wisdom of the first man relates to his long-range plan, which took into consideration the patterns of weather during different seasons throughout the year.

Though he does not use the same adjective, Luke's second builder seems even more foolish, as this person builds a house without a foundation (Luke 6:49). While other areas of the Roman Empire did not have sandy areas, the prospect of a flooding river was very well-known. Luke adds the detail about digging deep to emphasize the quality of the first builder's work (Luke 6:48). This builder was willing to put in the extra time and effort. He is not so much wise as he is hard-working.

Even in accounting for these differences, I do think we should keep in mind that both writers were trying to make the *same* basic point, albeit to different audiences. Sharon Ringe contends the Parable of Two Builders emphasizes a similar message in both Gospels: "The point is not to teach sound building strategies, but rather to make clear how life-encompassing Jesus' message is. What is needed to ground

1. Hare, *Matthew*, 86

a person in Jesus' teachings is to move from learning as an intellectual or emotional achievement to learning embodied in action."[2] Both Gospels preface the parable with references to *hearing* and *doing*, which highlight the importance of following the teachings of Jesus as a way of living. The implication is that *every* person needs to apply such wisdom to his or her own life, no matter where (or when) they live. I believe this point becomes even clearer when we consider this parable in light of other passages in the Bible.

Alongside Other Scriptures

Just like previous chapters have studied the same parable in different Gospels through comparison and contrast, we can engage in a similar method of interpretation with other passages in the Bible. This is known as interpreting scripture with scripture.

To begin, I've already mentioned this parable connects hearing the words of Jesus and putting his teaching into practice in one's own life (Mt 7:24; Luke 6:47). My colleague and mentor, Catherine Taylor, once pointed out to me that the Old Testament does not separate the notion of listening from taking action. In Hebrew, the verb for "hear" (*shema*) also means "obey." The most famous use of this verb is actually known as the *Shema* in Jewish tradition: "Hear, O Israel: the Lord is our God, the Lord alone" (Deut 6:4). The Israelites would have automatically known this injunction meant *both* comprehending and complying with the commands of God.

In a similar way, the early church took this connection for granted; in fact, this "hearing and doing" formula is explicitly taught in the Epistle of James (Jas 1:22–25).

2. Ringe, *Luke*, 97

The necessity of putting faith into practice is the key idea of perhaps the most famous passage in James: "Just as the body without the spirit is dead, so also faith without works is dead" (Jas 2:26). Earlier in the same chapter, the relationship between faith and works is presented as the duty to love your neighbor as yourself (Jas 2:8). This not only echoes the Old Testament (Lev 19:18), but is also a variation of the Golden Rule (Mt 7:12; Luke 6:31). Since human behavior, even attitudes, should reflect God's commands, faith is an action expressed toward the world and toward the rest of creation. That is a crucial understanding throughout the Bible.

In order to drive home this fundamental characteristic of the life of faith, the Parable of the Two Builders includes a stark warning. In both versions, the conclusion makes explicit the utter destruction of the house (Mt 7:27; Luke 7:49). John Carroll has noted this ruin is in complete contrast with sayings regarding "blessedness" found at beginning of both the Sermon on the Mount and the Sermon on the Plain (Mt 5:1–9; Luke 6:20–27).[3] Echoing certain themes we have discovered in other biblical passages, this parable mandates a faith that is intertwined with works. If you hear Jesus' words, then you must act in obedience. Not only are there no excuses, the consequences are dire.

This line of interpretation may seem obvious. But perhaps the underlying message is more complicated than simply doing what you have been told. One of the premises of this book is that Jesus told parables to push us into thinking beyond nice and neat moral platitudes. So like the builder in Luke, we must dig deep into our own lives in order to unearth more interpretations (Luke 7:48). Once again, we can discover gold by mining the content of other scriptures.

3. Carroll, *Luke*, 157

Recall that Matthew designates the first builder as "wise" (Mt 7:24). We have mentioned that this designation referred to his choice of location for his house, but reading alongside another biblical passage, I am reminded of Paul's understanding of wisdom as "Christ crucified" which paradoxically appears to be *foolishness* to the world (1 Cor 1:18–25). The point is that the wisdom of God can challenge the assumptions of our culture. For example, Matthew's Sermon on the Mount and Luke's Sermon on the Plain are full of "advice" that most successful people in our modern world would consider outright lunacy: turn the other cheek (Mt 5:39; Luke 6:29); if anyone wants to sue you for your coat, give your cloak as well (Mt 5:40; Luke 6:29); love your enemies (Mt 5:44; Luke 6:27).

These ethical commands seem illogical–even offensive–because we place such a high value in our culture on individualism: A penny saved is a penny earned. Pull yourself up by your own bootstraps. No pain, no gain. God helps those who help themselves. While nowhere to be found in the Bible, these "scriptures" are used by many people to interpret the parables and teachings of Jesus. But might our wisdom actually be foolish in the long run? Does our attitude of individualism create a foundation of love?

The subtle differences between Matthew's and Luke's versions of the parable imply that we, too, should apply the larger lessons to our own communities and situations. As we dig deep to listen and obey in our time and place, we must remember that Jesus often spoke, not only to individuals, but to a *crowd*. It is instructive to note that, while Matthew and Luke designate at the beginning of the Sermon on the Mount and the Sermon on the Plain that Jesus instructed his disciples (Mt 5:1; Luke 6:20), a great multitude was influenced by the end (Mt 7:28; Luke 7:1).

Clearly, none of us are gods. We all fail; we do not always listen or obey. Yet, by the grace of God, we can be part of building something than can withstand, not only the storms of life, but the consequences of our own mistakes that, like raging flood waters, threaten to wipe out our dearest relationships. In interpreting the teachings of Jesus for our time and place, Richard Lischer asserts, "When we as individuals fail . . . we do not snatch up cheap forgiveness, but we do remember that the [church] is larger than the sum of our individual failures and that it is pointed in a direction that will carry us away from them."[4] Instead of believing that everything is up to the individual alone, we can construct a home with others. By listening and obeying to scripture and to one another, we can become a family of faith.

Alongside My Son

Second Chances

I am a Protestant pastor, trained in the importance of grace, as opposed to works righteousness. But, as a father, it has become crystal clear to me that parents and caregivers shoulder a great and heavy burden of responsibility. The child comes into this world defenseless and dependent. Of course, taking care of him (or her) is our greatest joy! Yet it is up to the guardians to build a strong foundation on behalf of that child. Failure to do so results in all kinds of phobias and developmental delays. With the inevitable arrival of storms in life, most often we fall back on the type of behavior our parents modeled. Have we offered wisdom that will support and sustain those entrusted to our care throughout their lives?

4. Lischer, "The Sermon on the Mount," 161–162

When I was a young child, I remember eating lunch at the kitchen table with my father and brother. We were largely unaware of Mom, except when we asked her to bring us something else. We *were* oblivious, that is, until she slammed the dishes down in the sink and screamed, "Damn it, I am not your slave!"

Perhaps the greatest gift partners can give to their children is to model a loving relationship. This does *not* mean that everything will go smoothly. People make mistakes, which can result in fiery language. Compromises are forged in the white hot heat of conflict. It is precisely because of life's dramatic ups and downs that we need that solid foundation of love. My parents taught these lessons to me by how they reacted to that infamous day.

My father would be the first to say that he is not a god. But, to his credit, he tried to appreciate his spouse and spend more time in supportive roles with his sons. Growing up, I watched as Dad stepped up so that Mom could first go back to graduate school and then to full-time employment, following her life-long calling into a career in speech language pathology and early childhood development. The way that my parents aided and assisted each other through these transitions was not always easy, but it has left an indelibly positive impression on me. Hearing your loved one is important, but then you must make the necessary changes to build a life together. This, too, is a holy form of obedience.

Flash forward about twenty years to another heated argument in yet another kitchen. My wife, newly pregnant, pointed out our kitchen window to the sanctuary where I worked about three hundred yards away, and insisted that I was giving too much time and energy to my job. By immersing myself in my professional responsibilities, I may have meant well; but my misplaced priorities were, in fact, like those of a foolish builder. Ginny pointed this out in no uncertain terms: "Damn it, Andrew! You have nothing left for us!"

Maybe people assume that pastors and their families never curse at one another. But I thank God for my mom, for Ginny, and for other loved ones who are willing to speak words of judgment in order to refocus my attention upon the most sacred relationships. When Jesus uttered harsh invectives about complete destruction and utter ruin, I believe that he, too, spoke out of love. Sometimes a pointed word, even an explicative, actually shows how much you *care*. The disaster described in this parable is not what God intends or desires, but rather an honest look at the damaging reality of failing to arrange and order one's life according to matters of ultimate importance. I've taken this lesson to heart and applied it to my life, especially because of a specific aspect of our child's development.

Shortly before Sam turned six-months-old, Ginny and I began to introduce solid foods to his diet. I had always pictured this important step as involving a blender, which would reduce cooked foods to a puree so I could then spoon-feed my child. But Ginny discovered another means. With certain exceptions (notably processed foods, dairy products, and citrus fruits), we allowed Sam to try and eat pretty much anything on our plates. Let me re-emphasize the word, *try*. Especially at the beginning, he used food like finger paints, smearing it across tables, highchairs, and his face. Even when he managed to get a bit of food in his mouth, Sam was really just gumming it and sucking out the juices. His nutrition was still primarily from breast milk.

But we found this method of eating to be preferable for several reasons. For starters, we noticed that his hand-eye coordination improved almost immediately. Motivation is quite a teaching tool! In addition, he was introduced gradually to a variety of different flavors which, not so coincidently, were many of the ones that we enjoy. Today, he happily eats broccoli, asparagus, squash, hummus, wheat pancakes, sweet potatoes, and all kinds of fish. I don't think that he is ever going to be one of those children who will eat only French fries. He is a healthy, happy boy at least in part because we have laid a good foundation in terms of his eating habits.

Though all of these reasons are truly wonderful, what I value the most is that we eat together as a family. Sam seems to appreciate this dynamic as well. Often when someone places a piece of food in front of him, he will offer a beautifully genuine smile, as if he were returning the gift. Ginny and I intended to teach him some healthy eating habits; along the way, it seems that he learned something about *gratitude*–a "food" which nourishes his soul. Often he bursts into a spontaneous and heartfelt round of clapping at the end of a meal!

Of course, there are only so many hours in the day, and caregivers are responsible for putting food on the table. During the week, I don't always come home for every meal. But this act of eating together as a family has become foundational to our lives. And while my congregation is keenly aware of my faults, including the occasional sermon that falls short of providing spiritual nourishment, maybe my emphasis upon setting time apart to spend with loved ones "preaches" itself.

On the second Sunday of every month, families gather for an evening meal in the church's fellowship hall. From a storage closet, I pull out an old high chair, which hadn't been used in years. It has been given a new life–a second chance–as it is now Sam's throne from which he holds court, delighting youth and parents alike with his dinnertime antics. There are many other occasions when I am called upon to offer words; but on Second Sundays, I just sit back and watch, for building a foundation with food is the work of a community. Sometimes the better part of wisdom is silent gratitude for table grace.

Growing Smiles

The Parable of the Mustard Seed

AFTER WE FOUND OUT that Ginny was pregnant, she downloaded an application on her phone that gave us weekly updates about the size of the baby by comparing our child to food items. Yes, I realize this is rather silly; but every Friday, I would wake up eager to mark the growth in terms of the size of a new vegetable or fruit. Our baby grew from a poppy seed to a blueberry, and then from a sweet pea to olive. He was the size of an avocado, a cauliflower, a butternut squash and, finally, a watermelon. I will never walk down a produce aisle or stroll through a farmer's market the same way again!

My keen interest and impatience aside, it was clear that my wife did not need weekly reminders about the fact that our baby was growing. Only a month or so into the first trimester (when he was about the size of a raspberry) our little fellow started having a dramatic effect on her entire body. Forget "morning" sickness–Ginny suffered all day long. Her nausea began when she woke up and tried to choke down saltine crackers, and stayed with her throughout the day until she went to bed. On several occasions, I watched helplessly as she was reduced to tears, lying curled up in a fetal position on the couch. I did discover that it was neither useful nor supportive to point out this irony.

Of course, even with this discomfort, Ginny was overjoyed to be pregnant. Yet there were also some unforeseen consequences and difficulties. You can download all the pregnancy-information applications to your smart phone, but until you go through the experience, you really have no idea. We had to adjust our expectations and, as a result, learn more about each other and our relationship. Even as a tiny being growing in the womb, Sam had a transformative impact on our lives. Jesus described the kingdom of heaven in similar ways.

The Parable

Mark 4:30–32	Matthew 13:31–32	Luke 13:18–19
And he said, "How might we liken the kingdom of God or by what parable might we present it? As a mustard seed, which whenever it is sown upon the soil, is the smallest of all the seeds that are upon the soil; but when it is sown, it comes up and becomes larger than all the shrubs and produces great branches so that the birds of heaven are able to nest under its shade."	He set before them another parable, saying: "The kingdom of heaven is like a mustard seed, which a person took and sowed in his field. It is the smallest of all seeds, but when it grows, it is the largest of shrubs and becomes a tree so that the birds of heaven come and nest in its branches."	Therefore he said, "To what is the kingdom of God like and to what will I liken it? It is like a mustard seed, which a person took and threw into his own garden, and it grew and became a tree, and the birds of heaven nested in its branches."

Mark

A former professor, Carson Brisson, once explained to my class that we could think of the Gospels as written with Old Testament music playing in the background. Their focus is on the life of Jesus, but there are referents to the scriptures of Israel that the Jews in the original audience would have known by heart. As Jesus tells this parable, an ancient prophecy from Ezekiel can be heard in the background: the prophet envisioned a mighty cedar, growing tall on the top of the highest mountain (Ezek 17:22–24). This cedar represents the kingdom of God, re-established here on earth. The metaphor continued by imagining that all nations would stream to the holy city as birds nesting in its expansive boughs. These are powerful, lasting images of hope that the original audience would have known. "The kingdom of God is like," Jesus begins and, silently, people would have filled in the blank, like anticipating the punch-line of a familiar joke, *a mighty cedar on the top of the mountains of Israel.*

But that's not what Jesus says! The kingdom of heaven is like . . . a mustard seed? All of a sudden, the Old Testament background music comes screeching to a halt like a needle scratching across a record. Whereas the cedar tree was paradigmatic of power and might, the mustard seed in ancient Palestine was a *weed.* It barely grew to three feet tall. What's more, it multiplied rapidly, spreading out far and wide over the fields. What is the mustard plant, especially when compared to the glory and transcendence of the kingdom of God? It was more of a nuisance than anything else, like kudzu in modern day Appalachia!

Mark, in particular, seems to delight in reversing the expectations of the audience. He emphasized the diminutive size of the seed in comparison to "all the seeds that are upon the soil" (Mark 4:31). This hyperbole is reflected in other rabbinical writings that likewise use the size of the mustard seed for rhetorical effect.[1] (We do something similar in English when we say that something is the size of ant, even though there are smaller insects.) For Mark, the mustard seed was the metaphorical opposite of Ezekiel's mighty cedar. The text lacks mention of any tree, and emphatically states that a mustard plant grows into a "shrub" (Mark 4:32). *This* is the kingdom of God? Due to such cognitive dissonance, the parable must have been hard for the original Jewish audience to understand. Indeed that may have been Mark's point.

This Gospel places the parable almost immediately after the famous Parable of the Sower (Mark 4:1–9). In an aside to the disciples immediately following his public teaching of this parable, Mark uses the words of Isaiah to explain the purpose of parables: "They may indeed look, but not perceive, and may indeed listen, but not understand" (Isa 6:9–10; Mark 4:12). This emphatically underlines the harsh separation that Jesus defined between those on the inside and those on the outside (Mark 4:11). I'm told that jazz legend, Duke Ellington, once said that there are only two kinds of music: good and bad. For Mark, you either understood what the kingdom of heaven was like or you did not.

Matthew and Luke

In addition to employing the same words and images in the parable itself, Matthew follows Mark by placing the parable of the mustard seed in close proximity to the Parable of the Sower and Jesus' explanation about the purpose of parables,

1. Stern, *A Rabbi Looks at Jesus' Parables*, 54

including the quotation from Isaiah (Mt 13:1–15). By arranging the material in this order, Matthew and Mark have given the Parable of the Mustard Seed a polemic thrust. If one was expecting the kingdom of heaven to appear in a glorious fashion, like a cedar on top of a mountain, that person could easily miss the weeds that have sprung up all around his or her ankles.

It seems to me that Luke softens this contrast in the other Gospels between insider versus outsider. This Gospel does not describe the mustard seed growing into a "shrub" but a "tree" (Luke 13:19). In fact, some ancient manuscripts include an adjective that declares this tree was "great" in what must be read as an effort to echo Ezekiel's image.[2] Only Luke refrains from emphasizing that the mustard seed was the smallest of all seeds. Finally, notice where the mustard seed is sown: in a garden. While Fred Craddock may be right in that this location seems "very non-Palestinian" and therefore reflects an appeal to a Gentile audience, it is also true that a garden is a familiar, even comforting, image.[3] In subtle yet noticeable ways, Luke's re-telling renders the kingdom of God in terms that are less jarring of our expectations, more like music to our ears.

Another significant difference is that, while Luke does record the Parable of the Sower and the divisive quotation from Isaiah, he distances the Parable of the Mustard Seed from this material by five chapters (Luke 8:4–10). Instead he prefaces this parable with a public healing of a woman who had been unable to stand erect for eighteen years (Luke 13:11–17). In this narrative, Jesus is pitted against a leader of a synagogue who is indignant that a healing was performed on the Sabbath (Luke 13:14). The opposition is limited to this specific individual and the *people* are with

2. For example, see Luke 13:19 in the King James Version

3. Craddock, *Luke*, 171

Jesus. After the healing, "The *entire* crowd was rejoicing at all the wonderful things that he was doing" (Luke 13:17, emphasis mine). I know it's anachronistic, but can't you just imagine Handel's "Hallelujah" chorus playing in the background?

With Luke's decision to place the Parable of the Mustard Seed immediately following this public healing, the theme of the kingdom of God that confounds and overturns our expectations is still present, as a woman who was hurting for eighteen years is suddenly healed by the grace of God (Luke 13:13). And yet, for all its surprising nature, the kingdom is so fantastic that it is readily apparent, like crowds rejoicing and giving thanks to God (Luke 13:17). As a result of careful editing, the parable does not scratch the record of Ezekiel's background music but allows it to play softly. Jesus still puts a unique twist on the message, but the people "got it" just the same.

Conclusion

The function of a parable, wrote scholar Norman Perrin, is to "tease the mind into ever new perceptions of reality."[4] Jesus taught what the kingdom is *like*, not what it *is*. As we have realized in previous chapters, parables do challenge our perceptions, sometimes to make it clear that we have dearly held misconceptions about the way of God in the world. But, as Perrin continues, the simile is also *illustrative*.[5] There are lessons to be learned.

Despite their differences, it seems to me that Mark, Matthew, and Luke agreed on the most important teaching component of Jesus' parable. Even though the idea of

4. Perrin, *Jesus and the Language of the Kingdom*, 202

5. Perrin, 202

the mustard seed readjusts our expectations of a divine kingdom as compared to a mighty cedar, all three Gospels record another part of Ezekiel's prophecy: the birds of heaven coming home (Ezek 17:23; Mt 13:32; Mark 4:32; Luke 13:19). Scholars have noted that this is an inclusive image of hope.[6] As birds are able to fly across great distances to nest, so God's children will be gathered from the far corners of the earth. The key is that God will act, perhaps in ways that take us by surprise, but for the purpose of bringing us *together* in the same home. Despite all its mystery, we can nonetheless recognize the presence of the kingdom of heaven by the evidence of such unity. This is a joyful image; let the music begin!

Alongside My Son

A Sound Faith

Before Sam was born, I was unaware that babies must learn how to smile. I had visited several families in the labor and delivery wing of the local hospital and, while holding their newborns, witnessed a distinctive grin spread across the little one's face. Naturally I thought I was *very* good with children. Now I know that those babies were just passing gas! (This, in turn, makes me wonder how often I've congratulated myself on a particularly adept pastoral gesture when, in truth, the person was merely relieving a little pressure.)

My mother is a speech language pathologist with training in early childhood development. She told me that it takes babies several weeks to develop strength in the muscles around the mouth. Learning to smile was a matter

6. Williamson, *Mark*, 98–99

of physiology, but Mom said that I could "theologize" this if I wanted! So here goes . . .

We come into this world screaming, frightened, and confused. Then, as our muscles develop, we learn to smile. But I believe that this growth is more than just physical development. It seems to me that a smile is more than just reaction to external stimuli. It is the result of a strengthening of our capacity to trust. This evolution, however, is not as easy to measure as comparisons to increasingly larger types of produce.

From the day he was born, Sam had this habit of solemnly studying me for what seem like the longest time. He had the biggest, bluest eyes and stared at you like he was memorizing every aspect of your face, all at once, forever and ever. Then he'd have to look away, as if this sheer concentration was so exhausting that he needed a break. I told Ginny that he was a very serious little human.

But then Sam learned to smile and, once he started, has practiced this new skill more and more. He loves funny faces. He also delights at repeated sounds, like "la-la-la" or "sh-sh-sh" or, his favorite, "whooo!" One of the first times I ever saw him smile was in response to the alliterative phrase, "La leche! La leche!" Yes, the boy loves his milk!

Like other little children, Sam also adores being swung around or tossed in the air. One of the first times he ever giggled was when I balanced him on his feet on the kitchen countertop, a good five feet from the floor, and swung his hips around like a baby Elvis. I am afraid of heights and certainly wouldn't want someone standing me to close to a ledge in order to gyrate like the King. But Sam had learned something very profound from those early days of concentration: my son trusts me so unreservedly that he can literally laugh in the face of danger. You don't have to be a pastor to theologize the very best music to a parent's ears.

The kingdom of heaven is like a mustard seed that grows into a shrub. This is an improbable, if not downright silly idea, kind of like ridiculous faces and nonsensical things we say to babies to make them laugh. But the message is about *growth* in the truest sense–not only physical but spiritual–something like the development of a child's smile is also about cultivating trust. We first learn that others care for us, just for who we are, right at that very moment; sensing such love, we are able to open ourselves to receiving their gifts. Then we, too, are able to respond with love. Like waiting on a garden to produce vegetables, sometimes this growth is perceived through retrospect.

For those readers who are not Presbyterian, Montreat is a Presbyterian conference center in the mountains of western North Carolina that doubles every summer as the host site for six weeks of a youth conference attended by thousands of teenagers. In recent years, the location has also served college students during their winter break. Upon return from maternity leave, Ginny's first assignment as campus minister was to bring students from Virginia Tech to this four-day retreat. Naturally her immediate family had to tag along too. In addition to Sam and me, there were over a thousand students and adult leaders in attendance, which was the largest turnout ever! Sam was so completely wide-eyed during the experience of evening worship that he crashed afterwards. Indeed Montreat proved to be some of the best sleep that he got during his first three months of life.

I, too, had a couple of overwhelming moments, which I processed while lying awake and watching my little son sleep. I did not grow up Presbyterian, but had been coming to Montreat for almost ten years as an adult leader for summer youth events. During the college conference, I sat in the same auditorium and remembered a time, when I was right out of college and experiencing the pain of a particular break-up. Back then, I wondered if I was ever going to get married. A few years later with Ginny by my side, I once again worshipped in the same space as we hoped and prayed for a child. Now I sat with a wife and son whom I love even more than I could have ever imagined. Watching Sam sleep, I thought about how far I'd come and, in the dark silence of the night, whispered prayers of thanks like soft lullabies over his head.

The kingdom of heaven is like a mustard seed. It starts small, perhaps seemingly innocuous, before expanding beyond our wildest imaginations and blossoming as deep and abiding joy in our heart of hearts. Yet the kingdom of heaven may also require us to adjust our expectations, to realize that the plan of God is enfolding not exactly according to our time table. Such a realization is not always beautiful at first glance; it can require soul-searching and humility. But here's a truth I've learned: if we cultivate the kind of trust that allows transformation from within, not only do we find peace of mind, but the world outside seems less scary and the people we encounter less threatening.

I have tried to make the case above that the Parable of the Mustard Seed is more than just an anecdote about small things that can suddenly surprise us. Particularly in the case of Mark and Matthew, there is a polemical message that defines a community of insiders versus outsiders. You may not have thought about tensions between Jews and Gentiles in the original audience of the Gospels, but surely the idea of suspicion and fear between opposite sides of a religious dispute sounds familiar. Modern churches are prone to disagreement just like any other community of human beings. Too often people of faith lack a basic trust in one another.

Montreat is not perfect, although plenty of Presbyterians will tell you that it is a "thin place" where the division between heaven and earth seems almost permeable. People come from churches all over the country and, while the majority of the participants are white, there are other kinds of diversity: North and South, conservative and liberal, upper and lower class. In our denomination, we refer to the "big tent" by which we mean that such diversity is welcomed under the same roof. This notion is like the parable's image of birds coming from different places to make one home together. At its best, all the participants at Montreat are like the community formed in response to Jesus' healing: "The entire crowd was rejoicing at all the wonderful things that he was doing" (Luke 13:17). In other words, they get it. They understand that, despite their differences, they are united by their faith; they comprehend that their trust in God allows them to learn from one another. Could Christians be known for this? Could the church foster an environment like that?

Maybe such a movement could start small, like with a group of college students; imagine that this group shares a profound experience and the trust that they develop in one another would spread to other areas of their lives. They would share these insights and pass along these revelations, and the community would grow and expand across the country, as people of all ages matured in their faith. Sound impossible? Too naïve?

Well, like the very best jazz music playing in the background, that idea brings a smile to my face. Maybe to yours as well. And God has accomplished more with less before for the kingdom of heaven is like a mustard seed.

Hidden Threads

The Parable of the Yeast

I PASSED OUT DURING the birth of our son. Truthfully I hesitate to even tell the story because it seems rather ridiculous to draw attention to myself during the delivery process. But it happened. Just as Ginny began to push, I suddenly felt nauseous; then the hospital room began to spin. I sat down beside her bed on the floor and, the next thing I knew, was inhaling the strong odor of smelling salts! I looked up at a semi-circle of healthcare professionals and, as their faces came into focus, I realized they were *laughing*. One nurse later explained that my reaction is fairly typical. "You men just don't seem to be able to handle it," she chuckled, shaking her head at my gender's collective weakness.

In my opinion, no one who has ever watched a live birth should claim that a woman is a member of the "weaker" sex. It is a unique strength on display to bring a baby into the world. Though labor and delivery have been going on for the span of human history, it is no less remarkable each and every time. I might at add that it is still downright *terrifying*. I was overwhelmed at the amount of blood involved. I have never heard my wife scream like she did the morning Sam was born. I am thankful, however, that I was revived and able to stay in the room as a witness. While I believed ahead of time that I had married a strong woman, I will forever be in awe of Ginny after watching her give birth.

This chapter studies a parable about a woman who doesn't seem to do anything remarkable. She simply adds some yeast to flour, which is hardly worth getting excited over. Yet, as we shall discover, the strength of this woman inspires us to live into God's kingdom. In order to fully understand such a claim, we need to pay close attention to each key word in this very short parable. Mark Twain once said that the difference between the right word and the *almost* right word is the difference between lightning and a lightning *bug*. Let's take the time to encounter and consider the electric power of this text; hopefully no one will pass out!

The Parable

Matthew 13:33	Luke 13:20–21
He told another parable to them, "The kingdom of heaven is like yeast, which a woman took and hid in three measures of flour until the whole was leavened."	And again he spoke, "To what will I liken the kingdom of God? It is like yeast, which a woman took and hid in three measures of flour until the whole was leavened."

Matthew and Luke

Matthew and Luke transcribe this parable in almost exact verbatim: Jesus compares all the glory of heaven to wheat and bacteria in just one sentence. As we'll observe through a careful analysis of specific Greek words, Matthew and Luke seem to use the same "recipe" or combination of words to concoct this teaching. But along the way, we can notice the distinctive touches each editor employs by arranging certain material around the parable. It seems that a different combination of side dishes can actually affect the main course.

First, we have some translation issues. When English versions, like the New Revised Standard, state that the woman "mixed" the yeast, they are not following the literal meaning of the verb. Ironically, they are potentially "mixing" us up! In Greek, the word is a compound of the prefix, *into*, and the verb, *to hide*.[1] It is relevant to note that, immediately after the Parable of the Yeast, Matthew includes a citation from Psalm 78 to demonstrate that that parables are used in order to proclaim the mysteries that had been *hidden* or "kept secret" (Mt 13:35). My contention is that the same verb used twice in only three verses should be translated the same way, which justifies making explicit a notion of secrecy in the woman's actions.

This argument is further strengthened by the usage of the verb in other ancient texts. The Greek version of the Old Testament, the Septuagint, has several examples of "hiding" and these references are to some kind of secret concealment. For instance, a fellow named Achan took treasures from the Israelite camp and put them out of sight in his tent (Josh 7:20–21). We also find the words of prophets describing the futility of hiding sin from God (Hos 13:12; Amos 9:3). Unlike these Old Testament precedents, however, we must assume that the woman of the parable hides the yeast for *good* purposes, namely, advancing the kingdom of God. How, then, do we explain the secrecy?

As we search for meaning, let's next consider the object being hidden. In the ancient world, yeast did not come in bright little packages found in the baking aisle of grocery

1. Danker, *A Greek-English Lexicon*, 274

stores; it was made by storing a piece of bread in a dark, damp place until it had rotted and decayed. This is not a pleasant image, either back then or nowadays. Moreover Israel had equated unleavened bread with sacredness ever since the first Passover and subsequent flight from Egypt (Exod 12). By contrast, leavened bread was an every day, mundane occurrence.

In making an even stronger argument, John Dominic Crossan points out that yeast in ancient world was a symbol of moral perversion used as a metaphor for depravity in human behavior.[2] Jesus himself referred to the corrupting influence of the leaven of the Pharisees and scribes (Mt 16:11; Luke 12:1). Beginning in the third century of the Common Era, rabbis followed a similar train of thought by comparing the leaven in dough to the evil in a person's heart.[3] So either this parable "mixes up" the metaphor by depicting yeast in a positive light, or this somehow relates to the element of secrecy we identified earlier.

I contend that the person hiding the yeast is of paramount importance to solving such apparent contradictions. In an analogy to a more famous parable, the woman is to the yeast as the sower is to the seed. Indeed, take note that both parables are found in the same chapter in Matthew (Mt 13:1–9). Could it be true that Matthew in particular was intentionally trying to connect Jesus and the woman in this parable?

If that seems like a stretch, I would add that the verb employed by both Matthew and Luke, which means "to take," is the same word these Gospels use to describe what *Jesus* does to bread before the feeding of the five thousand and the Last Supper (Mt 14:19; 26:26; Luke 9:16; 22:19).[4]

2. Crossan, *The Historical Jesus*, 280–281

3. Stern, *A Rabbi Looks at Jesus' Parables*, 56

4. Danker, 583–585

We could frame the above question more specifically: Does the Parable of the Yeast insinuate that a woman could provide religious leadership? If so, this would constitute an attempted upheaval of cultural norms.

The household was the basic building block of ancient society in the Middle East. As a result, a system of roles defined and governed relationships between genders. Women prepared food, maintained living quarters, and most of all, bore children who enhanced the social status of the husband. By the time of Jesus, this social stratification in the home was reflected in the Roman Empire's advanced agrarian society. The public realm, such as government and commerce, belonged almost exclusively to men, while a woman's world was largely limited to the domestic sphere.[5] Think barefoot and pregnant in the kitchen; or, perhaps a woman stooped over from back-breaking labor:

Luke prefaces this parable with a healing miracle of Jesus specifically about a woman bent over for eighteen years (Luke 13:10–17). Clearly the major emphasis behind this narrative is the conflict between Jesus and a leader on the synagogue concerning the Sabbath. However, it is striking that a woman is mentioned just before this parable and that, through the power of God unleashed on earth, she is freed from her disease.

With both the historical background regarding women's roles and the liberating ministry of Jesus in mind, think about the significance of this parable occurring inside a home. The original audience would not have expected much from such a woman, especially if she operated in her customary sphere of influence. She *just* took some yeast and flour! This act has been done innumerable times by women all across the world. Who cares if she "hid" it or not? This is not a miracle, is it? What could be more ordinary?

5. Ehrman, *The New Testament*, 405–406

Actually this woman does something *extraordinary*. The amount of yeast used for three measures of flour would have produced far more loaves than even the largest of families could have possibly eaten before it spoiled.[6] Surely she must have been hiding something up her sleeve! In terms of the biblical record, she would have been in good company.

The Hebrew Bible is filled with descriptions of women who, by hook or crook, manage to pull one over on the unsuspecting men around them. Think of Tamar, who tricked her father-in-law, Judah, by disguising herself as a prostitute (Gen 38); or, Ruth who "uncovered the feet" of Boaz on the threshing floor and was betrothed to the wealthy man the next day (Ruth 3–4). Then there is Rahab, who hid the Israelite spies and, with a bold faced lie, sent the Canaanite police on a wild goose chase (Josh 2). I don't think it is a coincidence that Matthew includes each of these women in the genealogy of Jesus (Mt 1:3–5). God seems to be tied up with these women and their scheming plans, even their most dubious methods, as a means to achieve a larger, holier goal.

In light of this larger view of scripture, it is relevant to observe that both Matthew and Luke follow this parable with lessons about judgment. One Gospel records additional parables about crops and weeds (Mt 13:37–43) and a net full of fish (Mt 13:47–50). The point of each is that God will separate the good from the bad. The other Gospel envisions a fictive scenario in which some guests that are shut out by an owner who claims not to know them, despite their protests (Luke 13:24–30). This parable not only relates to the theme of judgment but also unexpected reversal: "Indeed, some are last who will be first, and some are first who will be last" (Luke 13:30). Because of the lessons that follow, we

6. Stern, 57

would suspect that the parable about a woman taking yeast might have a sharp edge as well.

To summarize, the parable describes an everyday household item, which was generally held to be unclean or impure, yet in this case was used by a woman in her daily life in such a secret way that it ends up having a huge impact. The message is hidden in the mix! The notion of a woman concealing the yeast implies the surprising, subversive function of the kingdom of God in our world, which works subtly and craftily behind the scenes. We don't have high expectations that anything significant will occur, but watch out! This is a recipe for the transformation of the larger society, one measure at a time, until the kingdom breaks into our lives in unexpected and astonishing ways. Pass out the smelling salts!

Alongside My Son

Trail of Hearts

While in line with the approach to interpretation of analyzing a parable found in multiple Gospels, the section above is unlike other chapters in that I have focused more on historical circumstances, rather than redaction criticism. I confess this belies a specific motivation: my wife, Ginny, is an ordained Presbyterian minister. Today our culture has made strides towards gender equality that would have been unthinkable in the ancient Roman world; yet women are still paid less for doing the same job as men. This double standard extends to the church as well. I have heard of the "stained glass ceiling," which denotes the unjust reality that women seem limited to certain positions of leadership, despite their skills and gifts. Sadly there are *still* denominations that refuse to recognize the calling of women into ordained ministry. I am not naïve enough to imagine that gender discrimination will no longer be an issue as Sam grows up. Thankfully his mother has provided courageous and inspired leadership even before he was born.

Both physically and spiritually, Ginny led our journey into seeking more aggressive infertility treatment. For months, I was saddened by our inability to conceive, but masked my anxiety with stubborn claims that everything would work out "just fine." On multiple occasions, I blithely told her not to worry about it. In retrospect, I think I was *terribly* worried that something was irrevocably wrong with either her or me. Thankfully Ginny paid attention to her instincts instead of my insecurity. She poured through medical websites in order to educate herself, and then sought out specialists, made appointments, even suggested treatments. Just as the woman of the parable took the yeast, she took *charge* of our situation.

Like yeast eventually spreads throughout the flour, Ginny's actions have also impacted the lives of others. Infertility is the kind of topic that you have to talk about with someone or you'd burst wide open. Unfortunately it is also a taboo subject in our culture and many people, including us, find it difficult to discuss openly. Grappling with the stress, we were caught between wanting to guard our privacy yet needing to share our feelings.

Once again Ginny led the way. She announced that she was going to start a blog with the poignant title, "Trail of Hearts: The journey of two hearts hoping to become three." In each of Ginny's heartfelt posts, she eloquently and honestly expressed her fears and hopes, frustrations and inspirations about the strange process known as in vitro fertilization (IVF). Initially the blog did not have a searchable public domain; but, after conception, Ginny gave the web address to our trusted fertility specialist so that she could share as a means of helping others along this journey. And now, Ginny has given me permission to share the link in the footnote below with even more readers.[7] Like yeast, her writing slowly works on the reader's mind until you, too, have been transformed.

Also analogous to the parable, Ginny's seemingly innocuous actions were in fact subversive of larger cultural norms, including some of what is taught in churches. I am aware that certain biblical texts "diagnose" the inability to conceive a child as the result of sin. I put this term in quotations because I don't think that the Bible is a medical textbook. I do know from experience, however, that people still use certain scripture passages as a sledge hammer to beat down those struggling with infertility. Men and woman are told that they just need to have more faith for God to answer their prayers, which implicitly and explicitly conveys that they are somehow unworthy. So hear me clearly:

While Ginny and I are thankful beyond measure for Sam, we also know good and faithful people are not able to have children. We don't pretend know all of the reasons why, but we are absolutely certain that it is *not their fault*. Instead of judgment, they need our support. This is the gift which Ginny's blog offers.

In one of her posts, Ginny was reflecting on this heartbreaking reality of infertility. She recalled that, while looking at an ultrasound, our beloved specialist had commented that her barren womb nevertheless looked like a *heart*. Talk about reframing a situation: the exact right word does have the power of lightning! When hope seemed to dim, we remembered this powerful simile and found the courage

7. Ginny's blog may be found here: http://trail-of-hearts.blogspot.com

to press on. We clung to our faith that God was somehow working in this situation in ways that we couldn't see, much less understand. For the kingdom of heaven is like yeast, which a woman takes and hides in three measures of flour until it leavens the whole thing.

Water is Wide

As a man and a pastor, I want to lift up Ginny's gifts and affirm the calling of other women as well. But this is only part of my responsibility. We also have to work as a team.

In terms of parenting, the importance of our partnership became paramount when we both went back to our jobs. It is one thing to share a single responsibility equally, quite another when potentially competing factors are at play. We try diligently to communicate and support each other both at home and in our careers.

Yet it is also true that we are not always team players. It is too easy to over-react to a minor incident or mutter a cutting remark at your partner. Some of our worst arguments during Sam's first year involved such trivial details that, honestly, I cannot even remember the cause of our dispute. But I will not soon forget how I made her cry. We know how to hurt the ones we know well.

I share these less than flattering details to avoid the false impression that my marriage is a paradigm of equality and harmony. Ginny and I love each other deeply; yet we are all too human, including our pettiness, insecurities, and anxieties.

And that's okay.

Particularly in light of the sharp edge of this parable regarding judgment, I want to underline the fact that Jesus told parables about ordinary items, like yeast, that became extraordinary in the hands of people, like the woman, *not* because those people were perfect but because they were *faithful* to the grace of God working through them. This theology, in turn, reminds me of baptism. Paul phrases this ideal so beautifully:

"As many of you as were baptized into Christ have clothed yourselves with Christ. There is no longer Jew or Greek, there is no longer slave or free, there is no longer male and female; for all of you are one in Christ Jesus" (Gal 3:27–28).

Though our society reflects the unjust reality of gender discrimination, our faith teaches that there is equality among *all* believers, including men and women, because of what *God* has done in Jesus Christ. Infant baptism especially reminds us that, even before we consciously know ourselves, God's unconditional love makes us a family of faith.

On Mother's Day, Samuel Greene Taylor-Troutman was baptized and "clothed with Christ" in a very special white gown. Gran, my maternal grandmother whose maiden name is Sam's middle name, made this beautiful garment over thirty years ago for my infant baptism. Decades later, Sam was able to wear the same gown because my mom widened both the collar and the sleeves. Though unable to make the necessary alterations herself, Gran had taught her daughter most of what she needed to know over the years. Just to make sure, Mom requested the assistance of a trusted friend from her church who had watched faithfully over the years as I outgrew the various clothes of my childhood and adolescence. Through so-called "domestic" acts with needle and fabric, these faithful women widened the thread of Sam's baptismal gown, which stretches across generations, time, and space. That meaningful household act of sewing continues to play a role in the kingdom of heaven coming to earth.

As I have reflected on the widening of the baptismal gown, Kathleen Norris reminded me that the Hebrew word for "salvation" literally means to make something wider.[8] Like a baptismal gown, our family is stretching because of our love for Sam. Often this is challenging and, occasionally, leads to conflict; yet he is always with us on our journey down "the trail of hearts." He reminds us of God's steadfast love and inspires us to be more faithful to our calling, more loving to those in our family, and more gracious to our larger community.

I think Jesus told the Parable of the Yeast for similar reasons. As the kingdom of heaven moves secretly in the most unlikely of places, slowly but surely leavening the whole, I hope that members of the community of faith can help one another glimpse God's grace. I pray for the day when our baptism truly unifies us, so that all churches will recognize gifts in men *and* women, even in the seemingly ordinary tasks we accomplish. If this vision seems too much and you start to feel overwhelmed, I know from experience that smelling salts are quite effective! Then you, too, can get up and begin to work as partners with those discerning the growing kingdom among us, perhaps lighting up our understanding with the right word at the right time.

8. Norris, *Amazing Grace*, 20

Sheep Dogs

The Parable of the Lost Sheep

THE IMAGE OF GOD as the Good Shepherd is one of the most beloved in all of scripture. One needs only to think of Psalm 23 and John 10. To that list, many would add the fifteenth chapter in Luke in which we find three consecutive parables about being lost and then found. Here, too, we read about a shepherd who rescues a lost sheep (Luke 15:4–7).

It has been argued that Luke makes this centerpiece of his message about God's amazing grace. Stanley Hauerwas states emphatically, "The parable of the lost sheep is not about us; it is about God's unrelenting love of Israel and those called to be disciples of God's son."[1] That is a beautiful, comforting idea.

The effect of such summary statements, however, has a tendency to conflate otherwise distinct images in different passages of scripture into a single presentation of the Good Shepherd in popular piety. To be clear, I am not attacking anyone's cherished belief! But a close reading of Luke's text alongside Matthew's lesser known version of the same parable will reveal some subtle differences for us to explore

1. Hauerwas, *Matthew*, 164

about the nature of God and the life of faith. Rather than feeling defensive, I believe that the uniqueness of each then allows us to emphasize the theology held in common. With this in mind, I invite you to think with me about lost sheep.

The Parable

Matthew 18:12–14	Luke 15:3–7
"What do you think? If a certain person has one hundred sheep and one of them is led astray, will he not leave the other ninety-nine on the mountains in order to go and search out the one that was led astray? And if it happens that he finds it, truly I tell you that he rejoices over it more than over the ninety-nine that had not been led astray. So it is not the will of your father who is in heaven that one of these little ones should be lost."	And he told this parable to them, saying: "Who among you, having one hundred sheep and losing one of them, does not leave behind the ninety-nine in the wilderness and go after the one that was lost until he finds it? And after finding it, lays it upon his shoulders and rejoices! And after coming home, calls together friends and neighbors, saying to them: 'Rejoice with me! Because I found my sheep that was lost.' So I say to you that there will be more joy in heaven over one sinner who repents than over ninety-nine righteous people who have no need of repentance."

Differences between Matthew and Luke

Since the introduction to this chapter warns about conflating the images found in the Gospels, you are doubtless anticipating an analysis of their differences. To begin, notice that the one particular sheep in Matthew "was led astray" (Mt 18:11–13), while in Luke it "was lost" (Luke 15:4–6). These translations accurately reflect different Greek words.

Matthew uses a verb that carries the connotation of making an error. As used in the passive voice in this parable, the word could even be translated as "to be deceived."[2] Luke, however, employs a different verb that, while translated as lost, implies something has perished or was destroyed.[3] The nuanced meanings of these word choices are highlighted by examining how the parable is used in the context of the larger narrative. It turns out there is more than one way of "being lost."

As previously alluded to above, Luke's message about "once lost and now found" is part and parcel of many people's faith. Think of popular hymns! John Newton's classic, "Amazing Grace," describes a conversion from a "wretch" into a saving faith, which is as dramatic as a blind person receiving sight. There is good justification for this interpretation: Luke prefaces three parables in chapter fifteen by informing the readers that "all the tax collectors and sinners" were drawing near to Jesus in order to hear him (Luke 15:1). This suggests Luke offers a message of universal salvation, even to those in a society who were considered to be lost and perishing.

Such an idea is controversial: Pharisees and scribes-subsequently grumble and complain that Jesus welcomes sinners and eats with them (Luke 15:2). These religious figures mistakenly make the story of the good news about *them*. As such, the parable functions in Luke as, not only a message of grace to those who are lost, but also a warning against hypocrisy to those who *think* they have already been found–the righteous who have no need of repentance (Luke 15:7). Despite what we may be tempted to believe, we should *not* claim that anyone is "lost" forever. God is the Good Shepherd, so we are not the gatekeepers.

2. Danker, *A Greek-English Lexicon*, 821–822

3. Danker, 115–116

In Matthew, this parable is in response to the disciples' question about greatness in the kingdom of heaven (Mt 18:1). The teaching that follows is aimed at the closest followers, not a gathering of sinful tax collectors and self-righteous religious leaders who, for all their differences, both come to Jesus as *outsiders*. So while Matthew offers his own rebuke, this warning is addressed to Jesus' *inner* circle. Instead of emphasizing the grace of God that reaches out to the lost sinner, Matthew instructs the followers of Jesus that they must be careful about their influence over others: "Take care that you do not despise one of these little ones!" (Mt 18:10). The admonition against "despising" literally prohibits the action of "planning against" people.[4] In light of their pursuit of glory and honor at the beginning of the chapter, Jesus prohibits his disciples from manipulating others in order to achieve greatness.

This reference to "little ones" is another major distinction. My initial impulse is to think of young children, like Sam. This would seem to be the dominant line of popular interpretation, as it seems as though every church nursery has a picture of the Good Shepherd on the wall. While it is Luke's shepherd who lays the lost sheep across his shoulders (Luke 15:5), this artistic depiction has relevance with Matthew's text. In his immediate response to their question regarding greatness in the kingdom of heaven, Jesus instructs the disciples to look at the example of a child: "Whoever becomes humble like this child is the greatest in the kingdom of heaven. Whoever welcomes one such child in my name welcomes me" (Mt 18:4–5).

But then again, Jesus taught adults as well as children, which might cause us to rethink exactly who was meant by "little ones." Scholars have purposed that the term could refer to *any* follower of Jesus who is especially vulnerable

4. Danker, 529

to deception, regardless of age. Douglas Hare, for example, imagines that Matthew could have in mind new believers, young Christians, or even "people who have no special gifts or charm." He contends that the term, little ones, is broad enough to refer to those, "Who are easily ignored in any group and who always remain on the periphery of the fellowship."[5] Regardless of whether or not one agrees with this conclusion, it is clear that the reference may be taken in a number of different ways, both literal and metaphorical.

This, in turn, directly relates to Matthew's distinction about being deceived or led astray. Those of us with power and privilege are not to take advantage of those who are vulnerable. There is nothing "great" or noble or virtuous about abuse or manipulation. The end result does not justify the means of how we treat others.

Conclusion, Part 1

It seems to me that the main difference between Matthew and Luke boils down to these concepts of "lost" versus "little." As such, this parable invites and encourages self-introspection. Do you feel, in the words of that famous hymn, like a wretch–a lost sinner who needs to be saved? Or, on the flip-side of the coin, are you grumbling and complaining about those whom God accepts and redeems? After studying Matthew's version, do you resonate with the reminder that a disciple strives for God's glory, not his or her own? Who are the "little ones" in your life who need love and support? Do you need to be on guard against using your position and influence in negative ways?

Undoubtedly people will answer differently, even in multiple ways, as your current situation in life will result in

5. Hare, *Matthew*, 211

identifying with one or more of these questions. But, while soul-searching can be an illuminating experience, I think that the parables also instruct our community of faith as a whole. This leads us to identify the characteristics and motivations that the versions hold in common.

Similarities in Matthew and Luke

Regardless of where we find ourselves, as sinners or righteous people, young or old, in positions of privilege or poverty, the over-arching goal of each version of the parable is the same: reunion with the ninety-nine. That's catchy sounding, isn't it? Sounds so great, in fact, that it is easy to sing! There is another classic hymn that reads, "There were ninety and nine that safely lay / in the shelter of the fold."[6] Like the mural of Jesus with the small children, that is a comforting image. The shepherd can go out and seek the lost all he wants as long as the rest of us are safe and sound!

But both texts depict a scenario that is far less comforting than this hymn would have us believe. One Gospel tells us that the shepherd leaves the ninety-nine on the mountains (Mt 18:12), while the other leaves them behind in the wilderness (Luke 15:4). While we once again find a different choice in words, each writer implies a similar idea about God, which then offers a similar *challenge* to the community of the ninety-nine.

In the Hebrew Bible, "wilderness" is a loaded word. It is the place where the Israelites were tested in their faith for over forty years. They faced famine and drought and numerous other hardships. They sinned against God many times, including the infamous idolatry of the Golden Calf (Exod 32). But the wilderness was also the place where

6. Ira D. Sankey, "The Ninety and Nine"

God came to the chosen people time and time again. God found them when they were *lost*. As stiff-necked and hard-hearted as the people could be, the love of God repeatedly and consistently triumphs over human rebellion. Therefore the wilderness is a place of despair *and* promise, of failure *and* forgiveness. As we have seen, this message is crucial to Luke's use of the parable to assert God's grace regarding those who are lost then found.

Also echoing the Old Testament, Matthew employs symbolic language about a geographical location. "Mountain" is another word that reminds readers of places where God interacts with people in times of trial. Moses met God on Mount Sinai after fleeing Egypt (Exod 19); Elijah experienced God's presence on Mount Horeb while on the run from Jezebel (1 Kgs 19). As Jesus gave his famous Sermon on the Mount earlier in chapters five through seven, Matthew surely intends to connect Jesus to these heroes of the Israelites' past, especially calling to mind Moses. I believe this effect compares positively to Luke's Gospel as well.

Even though they use different images of wilderness and mountains, Matthew and Luke share a theology concerning God's reconciling power. In both, the shepherd *finds* the lone sheep (Mt 18:13; Luke 15:4). Interestingly the reaction of the shepherd is also the same: *joy* (Mt 18:13; Luke 15:5–6). This is an amazing pleasure, so great that it cannot be limited to the confines of earth but is reflected into the heavens (Mt 18:14; Luke 15:7). The heart of this parable involves what Hauerwas termed "God's unrelenting love" that results in the reunification of the whole community, even during difficult times.

Conclusion, Part 2

Don't get me wrong: I am all for joy and reconciling love. Even so, this parable once struck me as completely counter-intuitive, if not downright absurd. Who would risk ninety-nine percent of his or her livelihood on the one percent that was stupid enough to wander off? Most of us make pragmatic value judgments based on totality. What makes us responsible adults is our attention to the big picture. We run the cost benefit analysis to our advantage, shrewdly cutting our losses in order to achieve prosperity. According to many societies in our world, getting ahead or on top is the reason to be joyful and celebrate with friends and neighbors.

So the parable's countercultural logic issues a direct challenge: whether in the wilderness or on the mountains, we are *exposed*. I hasten to clarify that I do not suggest God abandons us. But the downright disconcerting message is that the ninety-nine are *not* safely in the fold. It seems that God's seemingly foolish and reckless love places demands on us, pushes us out of our comfort zones and even challenges us to change our worldview so that we, too, might reach out in order to include others in our community.

Alongside My Son

Love, not Loss

I've met numerous people who refer to their pets as their "four-legged children" or "fur-babies." When Ginny and I were married, my dog became a part of our family.

We love Nikki dearly; yet were a little wary when we first brought Sam home from the hospital because our beloved dog is *jealous*. She barks at me when I give Ginny a hug! She was also up in years by the time our son came into the world, and everybody knows what is said about old dogs and new tricks.

At the very beginning, however, Nikki was *fabulous*. Almost immediately, she assumed the self-appointed role as Sam's guardian, placing herself before a visitor and barking loudly, even if the "intruder" was my mother-in-law. (Okay, maybe that behavior was less than "fabulous" but Nikki's instincts were noble albeit misdirected.)

But around Sam, this same "guard dog" was incredibly gentle, offering nothing more than a little lick on the back of his head or on the tip of his nose. She often slept beside him and, when he cried out, got up and nuzzled his cheek with her cold, black nose. If he continued to cry, she'd become increasingly agitated and give us this big-eyed, pleading look, as if to say, *For crying out loud; do something, will you?*

I found Nikki on the side of the road when she was a puppy, so while we don't have an exact way of knowing her pedigree, her interaction with Sam has confirmed our long held suspicion that she is some kind of collie. Shepherding comes naturally to her.

This sheep dog's relationship with our "little one" changed rather quickly. It all started when Sam began to figure out that those strange fleshy appendages flapping across his line of sight actually belonged to him. Once he discovered his hands, Sam would lie contently on his back and just stare, opening and closing his fingers again and again, utterly transfixed. But then he started to reach for things, including Nikki. He was very awkward at first, somewhat like a dog pawing at an object on the ground. But unlike canines, Sam has an opposable thumb, which means he has the ability to *grab*. With the development of this skill, our long-haired furry friend began to avoid this little creature who seemed to be constantly tugging and pulling on her.

No longer was she trying to shepherd him; now she needed protection *from* him!

What do you think? Is it possible to teach an old dog a new trick?

If I may use this question as a segue, it is popular and trendy nowadays in certain denominations to talk about how we want to welcome the "little ones" into our congregations by which we refer, not only to children, but especially to young adults and families. We also like to remind ourselves that we welcome the so-called "lost" in reference to those who previously have not been in communities of faith, the so-called "un-churched." Yet we often find ourselves biting off more than we can chew.

It is commonly said that people fear change; but I don't think that's the heart of the matter. Deep down, we fear *loss*. The presence of new people places demands on our ways of working and worshipping together. As others discover their calling and reach for positions of leadership, some of us feel threatened. We might slink away with our tail tucked between our legs or, even worse, bristle at the notion of change and want to bite back. There are, however, better ways to act and I do think we can train our thoughts and behaviors differently.

To this day, Sam absolutely *adores* Nikki. He basically learned to crawl because of his desire to reach her. Much to her chagrin, he learned to walk and now doggedly pursues her no matter how often she retreats. Occasionally she has become so upset that she actually started barking at him. Usually Sam just smiles back, blinking his eyes at the loud noise right in his face. He doesn't even mind if she knocks him down on his backside. But on a few occasions, she has nipped at him when he has yanked her fur too hard or tried to take away her rawhide bone. Though she's never really hurt Sam, Ginny and I were very concerned about these types of behaviors and, for a time, even considered separating the two, including the idea of banishing Nikki permanently outside.

I have asserted above that this parable about lost sheep is more than just a "feel good" message. There is a direct challenge: Can we form a fellowship of one hundred per cent? The parable makes it clear that such a community is exactly what God desires and causes heaven to rejoice; but it is difficult enough to have peace under one roof, much less one steeple. The idea of complete unanimity among all believers seems downright impossible in light of today's partisan politics and bitterly divided churches. We are tempted to think more realistically, as in, ninety-nine per cent is not half bad! Perhaps we would feel a little more safe and comfortable if we were more willing to cut our losses or push some of "them" out of sight and out of mind.

Yet, in so doing, might we likewise decrease our joy?

I do believe that God's unrelenting love finds what has been lost. When this happens, I am incredibly grateful and celebrate with all the angels and saints of heaven, including our four-legged friends. (Don't all dogs go to heaven?)

But I am keenly aware that most of us spend our days as part of the group of ninety-nine, trudging along through the wilderness, arguing as we labor up a mountain, and bumping into one another as we struggle to find our way forward as a large pack of individuals. Simply put, being in community is hard work. But the challenge reminds me of a saying by the fictional child known as the Little Prince: "Love does not consist of gazing at each other, but in looking outward together in the same direction."[7] The Parable of the Lost Sheep asks the ninety-nine to believe that such love is worth any effort.

7. Saint-Exupéry, *The Little Prince*, 55

Fortunately Sam and Nikki are learning to co-exist. So far, no one has been "lost" or banished from the house. Sometimes when Sam is badgering her, I can see Nikki's attempt at restraint waning in her dark eyes. At that moment, I'll suggest that we all go for a *walk*. With the mention of the magic word, all God's creatures spring up and bound out the door in the same direction. And believe me, there is great joy. Perhaps this is even a model for the church. We are more likely, I think, to have harmony when we are all participating together. Whether through the wilderness or up the mountain, it is good and holy to be moving in the same direction.

Holy Time

The Parable of the Wicked Tenants

LOVE, I THINK, IS deep and everlasting; attention, however, is a fickle thing.

In the days while I was still on paternity leave, Sam and I spent a great deal of time studying each other's face. I would rock him in the nursery and stare at this marvelous wonder in my arms. I noticed how much he looked like his mom and was very, *very* pleased! Meanwhile Sam studiously scanned my features, first focusing on my eyes, and then allowing his gaze to drift downwards to my mouth. It was clear that he was trying to figure things out for himself, including me.

When I went back to work, I couldn't help but notice that Sam seemed more attuned to Ginny. Perfectly logical: she was around him more often. But it stung a little. Then we hired a fabulous young woman who came to our house to watch Sam three days a week while both of our noses were to the grindstone. After she had been employed for several months, Sam would reach for *her* in the morning, even when he was in Ginny's arms! This stings a little too. I am keenly aware that, from the time he was three months old, Sam has spent more hours during a typical weekday with a caregiver than his parents.

In our culture, working parents often hear the phrase, "quality time with children." The idea is that the *nature* of the time a parent spends with a child is more important than the *length* of time. A shorter concentration of total attention is preferable to an extended session marred by distractions. Certainly it makes sense that having a ten minute, engaged conversation with a child is better for the relationship than merely being in the same room with the television blaring for a couple of hours.

By in large, I hold to this theory about the nature of time and have built "quality" moments into my day to be with Sam. This intentional practice takes some of the sting out of my necessary absences, and I suspect that the theory of quality time is partially attributable to appeasing the guilty consciences of working parents. To be clear, I do not dread schlepping off to the office each morning. I truly enjoy my profession and find ministry to be very meaningful. Yet the moments with my family are precious too. We speak of love lasting forever, but realize the time and space continuum in which events occur is limited and irreversible. Often friends, even strangers, will look at Sam with a wistful smile, "Oh, they grow up so fast. Time goes by so quickly."

Shortly before he was arrested and tried, Jesus told an audacious parable that all three Gospels frame as a direct condemnation of his adversaries. There seems to be little love lost between Jesus and the Jewish leaders. I believe, however, that this parable is really about the importance of time, specifically coming to terms with *God's* time as a particular period of abiding significance. So I hope that taking a longer look at this parable will be worth your while.

The Parable

Mark 12:1–9	Matthew 21:33–46	Luke 20:9–19
And he began to speak to them in parables: "A person planted a vineyard and put a fence around and dug out a wine pit and built a tower and leased it to tenants and went away. And at the right time, he sent a slave to the tenants in order that he might take out of the fruit of the vineyard from the tenants. But they took and beat him and sent him away empty-handed. And again, he sent another slave to them; and this one they beat over the head and insulted. And he sent another; and this one they killed, and many others, some of whom they beat, others they killed. He still had one beloved son. He sent him to them last, saying: 'They will respect my son.' But those tenants said to one another, 'This is the heir. Come, let us kill him and the inheritance will be ours!' And they took and killed him and threw him out of the vineyard. Therefore, what will the lord of the vineyard do? He will come and destroy the tenants and will give the vineyard to others."	"Listen to another parable! A person was a landowner who planted a vineyard and put a fence around it and dug a wine press in it and built a tower and leased it to tenants and went away. When the right time of the fruit drew near, he sent his slaves to the tenants in order to take his fruits. But the tenants took his slaves, and they beat one and killed one and stoned one. Again he sent other slaves, more than the first, and they did the same to them. Finally he sent his son to them, saying: 'They will respect my son.' But when the tenants saw the son, they said to themselves, 'This is the heir. Come, let us kill him and have his inheritance!' And they took and threw him out of the vineyard and killed him. Therefore, when the lord of the vineyard comes, what will he do to those tenants?" They said to him, "He will destroy those wickedly evil men and lease the vineyard to other tenants, who will give the fruit to him in their right times."	And he began to tell this parable to the crowd: "A certain person planted a vineyard and leased it to tenants and went away for a long period of time. And at the right time, he sent a slave to the tenants in order that they might give from the fruit of the vineyard to him. But the tenants beat him and sent him away empty-handed. And he provided another slave to send; but they beat and insulted that one and sent him away empty-handed. And he provided a third one; but they wounded and threw this one out. The lord of the vineyard said, 'What should I do? I will send my son, the beloved; perhaps they will respect him.' But when the tenants saw him, they discussed among themselves, saying: 'This is the heir. Let us kill him, so that the inheritance might become ours!' And they threw him out of the vineyard and killed him. Therefore, what will the lord of the vineyard do to them? He will come and destroy those tenants and will give the vineyard to others." After they listened, they said, "May it not be so!"

Mark

Someone planted a vineyard and leased it to certain tenants. When the right time came, this owner wanted to reap the profits and sent slaves, one after the other, to gather the fruit of the vine or the vineyard's produce. Yet they were beaten, expelled, and murdered by those tenants. Finally the landowner decides to send his *beloved* son, reasoning that he would be respected. But the very opposite happens! The tenants murder this son in order to claim his inheritance. In retaliation, the "lord of the vineyard" will destroy those tenants and give the vineyard to others.

Like the Parable of the Sower (Mark 4:2–9), most interpreters believe this Parable of the Wicked Tenants functions allegorically. Indeed its opening line, "A person planted a vineyard" is roughly analogous in ancient Judaism to the introductory formula, "Once upon a time" in our culture. The original audience would very likely recall the allegory used by the prophet Isaiah in which Israel is imagined as a vineyard that God planted, fenced in, and watched over from a tower (Isa 5:1–2). This story of the Old Testament, however, does not have a happy fairy tale ending: it is about *judgment*. Though God loved the children of Israel, they produced "sour" or "wild" grapes, thereby failing to respond appropriately to the divine gift (Isa 5:3–7). Apparently, the message of this parable is just as clear. Unlike the Parable of the Sower, Jesus does not need to explain this figurative meaning. Upon hearing this parable, the Jewish leaders fully understand the prophetic critique is directed at them and immediately want revenge (Mark 12:12).

In addition to this connection to Isaiah, we are led to believe that this parable is symbolic because the actions of both the owner and the tenants defy commonsense. No one would conduct every day business in this fashion. Gary Charles goes so far as to label these characters' behavior as "absurd."[1] I agree that it does not make sense to continue to send servants if previous ones have been beaten and murdered. In light of this abuse, who in their right mind would then send a beloved son? Not me! Likewise the rationale of the wicked tenants is almost comically ludicrous. The death of the heir does not change the fact that the property still belongs to the owner. It is not the case that an inheritance would automatically transfer to them. Their "plan" might as well have been concocted by Homer Simpson: D'oh!

Our serious efforts to interpret the parable, however, will once again be rewarded by side-by-side comparisons with other scriptures, as there are multiple allusions to the Old Testament in Mark's text. The "logic" of receiving an inheritance by getting rid of the favored son echoes the famous story of Joseph being sold into slavery by his own brothers (Genesis 37). Moreover the reference to "the stone which the builders rejected" (Mark 12:10–11) is from Psalm 118, a text which also imagines enemies surrounding the psalmist like angry bees (Ps 118:12). The key, then, seems to have more to do with ethical behavior than intellectual acumen.

Charles believes, "The violent action and corrupt logic of the tenants points to the violent and exploitative means to which stewards will sometimes go to maintain their privilege."[2] Ched Myers has argued robustly that this parable is part of Mark's condemnation of greed by those in

1. Charles and Blount, *Preaching Mark in Two Voices*, 193
2. Charles and Blount, 193

positions of power and privilege.[3] If the point is that these people exercise corrupt and immoral leadership, perhaps the implication is that wickedness has its own perverse logic contrary to God's perfect intention.

It seems to me that Matthew and Luke interpret Mark's critique of the authorities with subtle changes that further emphasize the contrast between the religious leadership in which Jesus encountered and the will of God of the world. Yet I will contend that Luke, in particular, provides a helpful corrective against a tragic theological misinterpretation.

Matthew

As a preface to further interpretation, the Gospels were written several decades after Jesus' death to "mixed communities," which is a term indicating the presence of both Jewish and Gentile cultures in the early communities of faith.[4] Jesus and his first followers were Jews. But more and more people from other religions and ethnicities joined this movement relatively quickly. Conflicts arose over the questions of maintaining these Jewish roots in light of new converts from foreign cultures.[5] It is commonly accepted in biblical scholarship that this later historical development is portrayed in the Gospels as a power struggle between Jesus and Jewish authorities. As is often the case, those with the most power also had the most to lose.

Through additions to Mark's text, Matthew magnifies a cultural clash in a mixed community by increasing the tension between Jesus and certain religious authorities. These adversaries promptly take the bait from Jesus and

3. Myers, *Binding the Strong Man*, 302–305
4. Franklin, *Luke*, 165
5. Senior, *The Gospel of Matthew*, 49–52

respond with an answer to the parable, which effectively renders their guilty verdict by their own admission (Mt 21:41). For a final jab, Matthew includes a closing line about the kingdom of God being taken away from some and given to others (Mt 21:43). While some translations obscure this meaning, the word referring to these new beneficiaries as "nation" or "people" also means "Gentiles." So it's clear that the battle lines are drawn; it is less obvious what a modern interpreter should do with this information.

Donald Senior maintains the decidedly negative portrayal of these Jewish leaders implies a significant percentage of Matthew's original audience was comprised of Jewish Christians, a category which refers to Jews who claimed Jesus as the Messiah and, therefore, were caught in a theological bind between a rock and a hard place:

> "On the one hand, the evangelist [Matthew] reassures his community that in following Jesus the promised Messiah and unique Son of God they were being completely faithful to their Jewish heritage and would find in Jesus' teaching and example the embodiment of all that God had promised Israel. On the other hand, the character of Jesus' own teaching and ministry, the decisive turn in the history of salvation effected through Jesus' death and resurrection, and the community's own experience of rejection by the Jewish religious leadership compelled the community to turn its future vision to the Gentiles."[6]

I've already highlighted this tension with past and present in my interpretation of Matthew's version of the old garment and new wineskins. Now nearing the end of Matthew's Gospel, this parable may well indicate a breaking point.

6. Senior, 84

With this in mind, Senior claims that this parable is of "fundamental significance" to Matthew's theology because it illustrates that the rejection of Jesus (the lord of the vineyard's beloved son) by certain Jews (the tenants) had paved the way for the inclusion of Gentiles (the ones who received the vineyard after the destruction of the previous tenants).[7] Reading the parable in this allegorical manner makes a certain amount of sense in light of the historical circumstances; yet might it have other drawbacks? What if we pushed the allegory too far, namely, by applying it uniformly to Jews and Christians today?

Luke

There is certainly conflict centered upon Jesus in Luke as well. Yet it is relevant to note that Luke downplays the reference to Isaiah's allegory by omitting specific descriptions regarding the building of the vineyard (Luke 20:9; Mark 12:1; Mt 21:33). This has prompted John Carroll to re-consider our text under the heading, "A Parable about Leadership Failure."[8] Carroll believes that, unlike Isaiah, Luke's image implies the destruction, not of vineyard itself, but rather those select people who are responsible for creating injustice.[9] The critique specifically involves the downward spiral of corruption by religious elites. Notice that Luke changes Mark's description of the erratic behavior by the tenants into a concise intensification of beating, dishonoring, and driving away (Mark 12:5; Luke 20:10–12). In other words, the longer those tenants have power, the worse their behavior. Carroll concludes, "A fruitful Israel under a new

7. Senior, 169

8. Carroll, *Luke*, 392–396

9. Carroll, 394

leadership group, not the rejection of Israel or the supplanting of Israel itself by Gentiles, is in view in the allegorical interpretive commentary pictured in Luke's rendition."[10]

Overall, the difference between Carroll's conclusions about Luke and Senior's insights into Matthew are subtle; but I think a nuanced understanding has important implications for modern faith communities. It is one thing to believe that Jesus' disagreement with ancient Jewish leaders resulted in his execution, and quite another to blame subsequent generations of Jews for his death. I am certainly *not* claiming that Donald Senior is guilty of this charge in his erudite commentary. But, tragically, history is replete with utterly horrible instances of blatant anti-Semitism and other grievous examples of Christians persecuting Jews. Specifically, supercessionalism is the term for a belief that Christianity has replaced Judaism, meaning the old religion is now condemned in the eyes of God. As a result, *Christians* have often acted like the wicked tenants by threatening, beating, and executing Jews in a frenzied mob seemingly drunk on power and high on corruption. Most, if not all, recognize this atrocity; but we need to take a further step and apply a similar logic to our biblical interpretations. We need to be clear and explicit about what we are *not* saying or even implying.

I learned this lesson from Amy-Jill Levine who is a top scholar of the New Testament. She is also Jewish. At the beginning of her lecture to would-be Christian clergy, she used to stand her young son in front of the class, bend down so she could put her arm around his slender shoulders, and ask those students not to advocate any teaching that would hurt her child. Now that I am a parent, her challenge is particularly convicting. I imagine Levine gazing at

10. Carroll, 394

her newborn for the first time just as I stared at mine. Of course she would want to protect him!

So, as I study this parable which supposedly condemns Jews and justifies Christianity, I want to highlight that each Gospel specifically cites Jewish *leadership*. Mark portrays a conflict between Jesus versus the chief priests, scribes, and elders; Matthew names the opposition as chief priests and Pharisees; Luke refers to scribes and chief priests (Mark 11:27; Mt 21:45; Luke 20:19). The overall point is the same: while their varying degrees of authority can be debated, these people constituted a minority of the total Jewish population. So we need not condemn an entire group of people for the actions of a few, either in first-century Palestine or our own time and place.

In our pluralistic society, this is particularly an important theological focus because our children are watching us. We need to model loving our neighbor, including those who are different. Since this includes the way we study the Bible and present its teachings, I want to highlight another aspect of this parable.

The Right Time

In reading of the Greek text, I have noticed that Matthew and Luke seem to emphasize another aspect of Mark: the notion of time. After introducing the parable, Mark tells us that the owner sent servants to the tenants "at the *right* time" (Mark 12:2, emphasis mine). I have consistently applied this adjective, right, to modify the word, time, in order to reflect a translation. Unlike English, there are *two* words used in the Greek New Testament for "time." *Chronos* refers to time that is quantifiable, as in the duration of an activity or event. It can be either long or short, but always refers to time with a fixed beginning and ending.[11] It may be helpful to note that English derives the word, chronological, from this sense of time. *Kairos*, which I have translated as "right" time, lacks the same emphasis on *quantity*. Instead the focus is on the *quality* of the experience, whether positive or negative. Most often, *kairos* time is a period characterized by special circumstances, especially relating to the divine plan or even a direct experience of God.[12]

As you can verify by my translations above, each Gospel follows Mark's use of *kairos* time. Luke even draws a specific contrast, stipulating that the owner went away for "a long period of time/*chronos*" and "at the right time/*kairos*" sent the slaves to collect the produce (Luke 20:9–10). This is an excellent illustration of the difference of terms: in terms of his absence, the point is about a period of duration; but when it comes to the harvest, the emphasis is on that unique moment.

Matthew amends Mark's text to read, "When the right time/kairos of the fruit drew near," which, allegorically speaking, references the long awaited moment of the coming of the Son of Man and the fulfillment of God's reign on earth. (We will encounter this theology in more detail in a later chapter.) Also in Matthew, the opponents recognize that a crucial moment in time is the fundamental issue at stake. In response to Jesus' question about what the owner will do, they reply that the new recipients "will give the fruit to him in their right times" (Mt 21:41). I realize this translation is awkward; but I am suggesting that relating a sense of *kairos* time is more fundamental to the interpretation than smooth English. The "right" time is everything.

11. Danker, *A Greek-English Lexicon*, 1092

12. Danker, 497–498

Here's the larger point: the way we understand time relates to how we treat others. If we were correct in stating that the parable condemns those leaders who exercise the perverse logic of power and exploitation, then the inverse is also true, namely, that true leaders see the world in God's terms of justice and righteousness. This "*kairos* attitude" could be summed up by another part of the same psalm quoted in this parable: "This is the day that the Lord has made; let us rejoice and be glad in it" (Ps 118:24). If the rejection of Jesus as the cornerstone is the verse to interpret the negative behavior, then I would suggest that this other verse holds the key insight for positive ethical action. It's now time for me to give an illustration!

Alongside My Son

Lessons from Mom

Ginny and I first met Sam at 12:52 p.m. on October 25th, 2012. But, of course, that sacred moment was not frozen in time. We couldn't stay in the hospital surrounded by incredible nurses who attended to our every need. Eventually we had to go home. As I recall, there was plenty of nervousness to go along with our excitement.

Our first night with Sam, I slept about two and a half *minutes*. Perhaps Ginny managed to rest a little more. I do know that, every time our newborn would so much as sigh in his sleep, one of us would spring out of bed and anxiously peer into the bassinet. Once, upon finding him still sound asleep, I actually poked him just to be safe. Rest assured that he was alive; in fact, he started yelling at me. (I'm quite sure that Ginny was tempted to do the same!)

On that first night, Sam certainly did not need any pokes or prods. He woke up frequently on his own, frantically scanning the room with those big eyes and crying loudly. Can you even imagine what it must be like to wake-up as a newborn, so unfamiliar with *everything*? Well, that sleepless night was not the time for abstract thoughts; something practical had to be done. About 4:30 in the morning, my wise wife had a brilliant idea: "Why don't you see if your mom would watch him for a few hours?"

To some, this suggestion would imply that she thoroughly detested her mother-in-law! So you should know that, just before bed, Mom told us to come and get her if she could be of any help. So that's exactly what I did, trudging downstairs and wearily knocking on the door to the guest bedroom. Apparently she wasn't sleeping that well either, for she immediately answered with her eyes full of concern.

"Mom," I pleaded, "Can you watch Sam for awhile?"

The worry melted from her face.

"Oh honey! I'd love to."

Thank God, Mom took this early morning shift! But as much as it meant to our sanity, the experience was even more meaningful to her. Later, she described how she was fully awake and completely present to Sam's every move, as if she could see his personality outlined like a halo in the faint light of the nursery. As the sun came up and he gradually stirred, she told him how much he was loved. When I came back and asked about the experience, Mom said that those two to three hours flew by for her as if they were a mere matter of moments. And I'll never forget what she said: "This was a *holy* time."

This description perfectly illustrates the difference between the two types of time we've described in the New Testament. *Chronos* has to do with measurable time, the minutes ticking into hours between four and six in the morning. *Kairos* refers to Mom's experience of time as *immeasurable*, as sacred and precious moments that somehow transcend the clock. I've carried her experience of holy time with me.

Sometimes I do feel guilty about punching the time-clock at work. So what I do with *chronos*, I try to make up with *kairos*. Almost every morning, I hear Sam babbling over the baby monitor and creep into his room. "Who's is awake in here?" I whisper, and then, raising my hands with a dramatic flair, "It's the *Sam-man*!" He gives me a big smile. As I undergo the routine task of changing his diaper, we sing songs. Some are familiar nursery rhymes and others I've made up with very silly words. Sam coos right along to both. The music is less about passing the time and more about enjoying these few minutes together. With the early morning light streaming into the nursery and illuminating my beloved son, I am fond of singing a fittingly titled Bob Dylan song, "Time Passes Slowly." Sam often responds to this tune with nasal grunts that I swear sound just like the famous musician himself! It is holy time.

The Parable of the Wicked Tenants issues a poignant charge to those who have been entrusted with the care of others. No honest interpreter can explain away the judgment that is explicitly stated for those who, regardless of religion or ethnicity, abuse their power to hurt the vulnerable. Wickedness has its own perverse logic contrary to God's perfect intention.

But I do not encounter such wicked behavior on a regular basis. More often, I meet people who, upon seeing Sam, lament that their own children or grandchildren or great-grandchildren have grown. Sometimes they say, "Don't you just wish they stayed this age?" But I once heard my mom comment that she didn't have a favorite age: "What matters, Andrew, is the time you get to spend with your children."

So I've come to believe another challenge of the parable is to appreciate what we have been given, whether a vineyard or a relationship, not because it could be taken away, but since it is ours to *share*. A desire for "quality time" is a good start; yet I hope that we can push further and go deeper because our understanding of time really does impact they way we treat others. I believe that we are called to make the most of the *kairos* moments we have to love others, no matter how old or how young. For this is the day that the Lord has made; let us rejoice and be glad in it.

Healthy and Strong

The Parable of the Great Banquet

If I may say with more than a hint of pride, Sam is incredibly strong. In the colloquialism of the Appalachian Mountains, the boy's a biggin.' Upon stepping into the waiting room, moments after delivery, our midwife jokingly informed my parents, "Congratulations, you are the proud grandparents of a toddler."

There was hardly a time when this big guy was completely immobile either. After only a few days, he could lift his head off your shoulder and turn to face the other direction, a display of neck strength which is pretty remarkable for a newborn. From a very young age, he also displayed a ferocious grip. When I was trying to help him battle through a fussy spell, Sam would grab the collar of my T-shirt and actually stretch it to resemble a V-neck. While I've already mentioned is ability to flail his arms out of the tightest swaddle, I'll add that, if unhappy, he would arch his back and threaten to kick himself right out of your arms.

As Sam grew, we watched with great delight as he explored the world around him with all of his might. Very quickly he was sitting up on his own, which freed his hands to grab anything within reach. Before we knew it, he was leaning forward, slowly but surely starting to scoot and crawl towards the object of his desire. He began pulling himself to a standing position, very unsteadily at first but gradually becoming more solid with his chunky thighs like tree trunks underneath him. He next began to cruise around ottomans and coffee tables, holding on with his own hands. About this time, we discovered that he took great delight when we grabbed his hands and "walked" him around. Before his first birthday, Sam was walking by himself.

As his father, I was thrilled about this relatively early development of a major milestone: "That's my boy! Look at him go!" But my enthusiasm was quickly curtailed by the realization that his newfound mobility now put him in harm's way. Anyone who has ever "child-proofed" a house knows exactly what I am talking about. Never before had a simple electrical outlet appeared so sinister, a staircase an outright death trap. I realize that we are very fortunate, not only because Sam walked early in life, but because he is healthy and strong. I wouldn't have it any other way; yet these blessings entail a great sense of responsibility too.

Matthew and Luke record a parable that reminds me of these themes, especially in light of the famous axiom, "Many are called, but few are chosen" (Mt 22:14). While we'll discover some important differences, I think both Gospels challenge us to understand true strength as mutual accountability to a larger community, instead of power over others. Therefore we may have to check our egotistical satisfaction at our own achievements in order to be a part of something truly worthy of our best energy–God's kingdom on earth.

The Parable

Matthew 22:1–14	Luke 14:16–24
By way of answering, Jesus again spoke to them in parables, saying: "The kingdom of heaven may be likened to a king, who made a wedding banquet for his son. And he sent his slaves to invite the ones who had been invited to the wedding banquet, but they did not want to come. Again he sent other slaves to say, 'Speak to the ones who have been invited: Look! I have prepared my meal, my bulls and fat calves have been slaughtered, and all is ready. Come to the wedding banquet!' But they were unconcerned and went away, one into his own field and one to his business; and the rest seized his slaves, mistreated and killed them. The king was enraged and sent his soldiers to destroy those murderers and burn their city. Then he said to his slaves, 'The wedding banquet is ready, but the ones who had been invited were not worthy. Therefore go to the highways and, whoever you should find, invite to the wedding banquet.' And those slaves went out into the highways and gathered together all whom they found, both wicked and moral; and the wedding banquet was packed with guests. But when the king came in to see the guests, he saw a person who was not dressed in clothes for a wedding. And he said to him, 'Sir, how did you enter here without having clothes for a wedding?' But he was silent. Then the king said to the waiters, 'Bind his feet and hands, and throw him out into the outer darkness!' Weeping and grinding of teeth will be there for many are called, but few are chosen."	Then [Jesus] said to him, "A certain person made a great banquet and invited many people. At the hour of the banquet, he sent his slave to tell the ones who had been invited, 'Come on, because now it is ready.' But every one of them began to make excuses. The first said to him, 'I bought a field and I must go and see it. I ask you, have me excused.' And another said, 'I bought five teams of oxen and I am going to approve them. I ask you, have me excused.' And another said, 'I married a woman and because of this, I am unable to come.' The slave returned and reported these things to his lord. Then the master of the house grew enraged and said, 'Go out quickly into the streets and roads of the city and lead the poor and the crippled and the blind and the lame in here!' And the slave said, 'Lord, what you commanded has been done, and yet there is still room.' And the lord said to the slave, 'Go out into the highways and lanes and compel them to come in so that my house might be full. For I say to you that not one of those men who had been invited will partake of my banquet.'"

Luke

A certain person threw a large dinner party commonly referred to as a banquet. From this festive beginning, however, the narrative quickly sours. Those who have been invited beg off for different reasons: one has to see about a field, another to his livestock, and a third has just been married. The host is absolutely enraged! But aren't these legitimate excuses? What prompts this angry response? After all, the guests are even polite (Luke 14:18–19).

I am indebted to a former professor, John T. Carroll, for shedding light on such questions. He notes that the host initially invites his social peers: an absentee landowner, a proprietor of a large farm, and a gentleman who can afford social obligations. In a world where the vast majority of people were subsistence farmers, these are people with considerable means. So their feigned politeness is actually a "conspiracy of last-hour refusals" designed to shame the host.[1] He is being shunned by a collected effort from high society, which implies that their absence is really a backhanded attack to lower his status. No wonder he's furious!

More importantly, if we read the parable through this lens of class, then we understand the profound significance of the host's next move to extend the same invitation to those living in the streets and roads of the city. Much like today, ancient cities were populated with urban poor who were unable to work because of physical ailments, i.e., the poor, the crippled, the lame, and the blind (Luke 14:21). Just outside the city, beggars congregated in the highways and lanes that led into the marketplaces (Luke 14:23).[2] These people were supposed to "know their place" and stay there too. But in response to the snub by the rich and

1. Carroll, *Luke*, 303
2. Carroll, 304–305

powerful, the host turns his society's system of privilege on its head. By inviting members of the lower class, he refuses to play by the rules that define economic status and social privilege. Therefore the host implicitly calls into question the morality of elites who gain their affluence at the expense of the masses.

When Brian K. Blount was reading a draft of this chapter, he noted the irony that the host only performs this moral action for strangers after he was treated so *immorally* by his acquaintances. Just as Sam's ability to walk caused me to look at our house differently, new experiences allow us to see things (even about ourselves) we hadn't considered before.

In this case, the unexpected actions of the host open his eyes to the Gospel message. Jesus prefaces this parable with instruction to his followers to invite the poor, the crippled, the lame, and the blind to their banquets (Luke 14:13). This is the exact *same* guest list found in the parable! Often parables are interpreted allegorically, but in this case, a literal interpretation is clearly intended. This understanding is utterly consistent with Jesus' earlier statement, "Blessed are the poor" (Luke 6:20). Notice that Luke does not have Matthew's modifier, "Blessed are the poor *in spirit*" (Mt 5:3, emphasis mine). Reading Luke's version for what it says, the host is a person of privilege who uses his means on behalf of others in need. If such thinking sounds like a wasteful or ineffective means of conducting business or social-networking, then perhaps the message is to focus on different objectives or standards of success. Your payment is not in this life but at the resurrection (Luke 14:12–14).

To summarize, the parable in Luke's telling challenges the monetary system of his culture, which was based on rubbing elbows and scratching backs as a means to secure one's place at the top of the social ladder and, by extension, ensure that other people remain at the bottom. A culture, I might add, which should sound awfully familiar to those of us living in the United States of America.

Matthew

Unlike Luke, Matthew introduces our parable with the familiar refrain about comparing the kingdom of heaven to something else, so the reader is already prepared for symbolic language. And Matthew does not disappoint, informing us that a certain king prepared a wedding banquet for his son (Mt 22:2). Symbolic images were often used to envision and represent the messianic kingdom by which a king (representing God) has prepared a wedding banquet (paradise or heaven) for the son (the Messiah or Anointed One) and certain wedding guests (the believers or disciples). In light of these symbols and the theology they represent, we would expect a scene of judgment, which is exactly what we find. Those who were originally invited were either too busy with their own properties or businesses or, even worse, abused and murdered the slaves of the king (Mt 22:5–6). Subsequently the king destroys them and burns their city because they were not "worthy" (Mt 22:7–8). Afterwards, those out in the highways are invited to the same feast (Mt 22:9).

While the basic plot accords with Luke's version, the highly symbolic language of a "wedding" banquet suggests a different interpretation. As we consider the larger narrative, Matthew's position of the parable in his Gospel belies a distinctive purpose. Particularly because this parable follows the expulsion of merchants from the Temple (Mt 21:12–13) and the Parable of the Wicked Tenants (Mt 21:33–44), many interpreters explain this parable as an allegorical interpretation of salvation history. Originally designated as God's chosen people, Israel has failed to keep the covenant or their end of the deal. As punishment, the Temple was destroyed. Now God has extended the invitation to the Gentiles. Bearing in mind the caveat from the previous chapter about supercessionalism, this explanation is nice and neat, logical and straightforward. We might be tempted to wrap things up right here . . . except the text *continues*!

The parable pivots with the ominous note that both the moral *and the wicked* were invited to the feast (Mt 22:10). Why were evil people allowed to participate in the king's celebration? Their inclusion sets the stage for another judgment, as the king himself confronts a guest who is not dressed in the proper wedding attire. Many translations preface the king's question with the term, "friend" or "comrade" (Mt 22:12), but the word in Greek does not necessarily imply a positive relationship, rather a general form of address to a stranger.[3] In this case, I have chosen to translate the word as "Sir" to avoid confusion. However, the larger point is that, while the king does not know this guest personally, he nonetheless holds him accountable to the dress code. Apparently the stranger's silence is indicative of his guilt and he is thrown into the outer darkness (Mt 22:13). Reading this allegorically, a wedding garment symbolizes repentance and good deeds. Therefore Donald Senior writes, "Matthew's theology is utterly consistent: the same criterion of repentance and good deeds is applied to both Jews and Gentiles . . . the Gentiles are not a privileged class who take over from Israel . . . Belonging to God's people means doing the will of God."[4]

If the first half of the parable served as a warning to Israel, the second portion is addressed to other nations. The

3. Danker, *A Greek-English Lexicon*, 398

4. Senior, *The Gospel of Matthew*, 155

contrast between "moral and wicked" echoes the earlier parables about "wheat and tares" (Mt 13:24–30) and a net full of "good and bad" fish (Mt 13:47–50). All of these metaphors imply Matthew's theological conviction that the gracious invitation of God does not alleviate the responsibility of our faithful response, whether Jew or Gentile.

Just because this teaching is clear, however, does not mean that it is easy to obey, as the concluding verse famously warns, "Many are called, but few are chosen" (Mt 22:14). "As Christians," claims Stanley Hauerwas, "Our task is like that of the chief priests and Pharisees: to be able to recognize ourselves in the parables."[5] But we have a convenient way of interpreting ourselves *out* of the parables. Certain conservative movements have a long, sad history of supercessionalist theology, which derides the Jews for their lack of faith, thereby implicitly and explicitly making the case that Christians are superior by default. On the other side of the same coin, Hauerwas claims that this parable "makes for uneasy reading" for more liberal Christians "who want Jesus to underwrite a general critique of elites in the name of creating a community of unconditional acceptance."[6] It seems many Christians–evangelical and progressive and whichever labels one wishes to use–make the mistake of asserting that Jesus came to judge *others*, not them.

In Matthew's telling, our parable begs to differ. It mandates a high level of accountability: belonging to God's people mandates doing the will of God in one's own life. We are required to walk the walk, or in light of the image of the wedding garment, dress the part.

5. Hauerwas, *Matthew*, 188

6. Hauerwas, 189

Conclusion

Though I have contended that Luke's version was intended to be applied more literally, while Matthew's parable is best understood as allegorical, it seems that the desired effect upon the reader is very *similar*. The parable, according to Carroll, is "a cautionary corrective" because "participation in the banquet of God's realm indeed conveys blessing, but one should not presume to have a secure place at that table."[7] Neither social status nor power nor wealth, neither ideology nor worldview, and not even religion serve as justification in the kingdom of God. Taken together, Matthew and Luke teach us that how we treat others is a reflection of our faith. Believing that God graciously invites us, we should strive to do the same to others, regardless of what they can give us in return or if they hold the same politics or beliefs. According to both versions of the parable, it is our response to the grace first given that makes us makes us "worthy" to be guests in the kingdom of heaven.

As I have hinted throughout this analysis, this interpretation is countercultural to the American ideal of individualistic success and current reality of partisan politics. Instead, Jesus offers an invitation to something else, which is clearly another way of life. In both Gospels, this parable reminds us that the best party is thrown, not by humans, but by *God*. Such divine graciousness, in turn, forms a sacred guest list: a community based on mutual respect and self-giving love. Again, this is easy to say and difficult to do. As I wrestle with such challenges, my experience of parenthood has taught me something about a gracious faith that might best be termed, *healthy*.

7. Carroll, 301

Alongside My Son

A Kiss of Peace

Upon meeting us at the hospital in the wee hours of the morning after Sam's birth, our pediatrician promptly informed us, in no uncertain terms, that our baby should not be allowed in public places for at least eight weeks. *Eight* weeks! I looked at Ginny and saw a mirror of my own exhausted disbelief. Had we heard him correctly? When I turned back incredulously, the doctor informed us that a newborn essentially lacks an immune system. Upon later reflection, that claim still seems as counterintuitive to me as in that initial moment. Evolutionary speaking, you would think that our species would have built up some resistance over the great span of human history. Then again, viruses, like the flu, are constantly evolving too . . . I'll leave this debate to the scientists and medical professionals.

One thing I know for certain was this mandate fed my anxiety. In the coming weeks, I obsessively washed my hands to the point in which they became dry and brittle like the dead tree limbs littering the cold winter ground of southwestern Virginia. When I came down with a stomach virus, I not only slept in another room, but on another *floor* of our house. To this day, Ginny contends that I literally worried myself sick.

I, however, take a measure of comfort in that I am not alone in practicing such hyper-vigilant behavior among first-time parents. I remember, when our friends brought their firstborn home, they all but *attacked* us with hand-sanitizer before we even walked through their door. (Alright, maybe identifying such people is not much of a comfort after all.)

If one is not careful, a parent's mantra might be, "Stay away from human contact." I think we could all agree that such a belief is problematic, not the least of which because following this practice is downright impossible. Especially if one is the pastor of a small, rural congregation.

While we were gamely enforcing the mandated eight-week isolation period, there were elderly women at church who, upon seeing me, would forgo any semblance of good Christian restraint and exclaim, "I can't wait to get *my* hands on *that* baby!" Inevitably she would then sneeze and promptly wipe her nose with the back of her hand. And I, without any semblance of good Christian hospitality, would mutter very quietly to myself, "*Whose* hands on *my* baby?"

As a general rule, Ginny is less anxious than me; but we both wanted to take the necessary and proper precautions. We certainly do not actively court danger or illness. The longer I am a parent, however, the more I realize that I am not in control of Sam's life anymore than my own. In their own time, children are going to learn to move and explore the world around them. You can keep your son or daughter locked away in your perfectly child-proofed house and, God forbid, still have a tragic accident or fluke illness. Experience eventually teaches that the idea of a germ-free environment or risk-free space is simply an illusion–more specifically, a self-*delusion*. Our hand-sanitizing friends just had their fourth child and I seriously doubt we'll get the same Purell treatment this time around.

One reaction to the fragility of life is driven by anxiety and may culminate in outright fear, as we try and close ourselves off from people. A more faithful response reflects the lesson of our parable, especially Luke's version. We *want* people to get their hands on us. So we make an effort to come into contact with others, even those who are sick and dirty and poor. Of course, this risks exposure to germs; but Jesus taught that "catching" or "coming down with" such *love* is the very hallmark of the kingdom of heaven on earth.

After his mandated period of limited human contact had expired, Sam regularly attended worship services and other church functions to the utter delight of my parishioners. At each event, he was held and hugged, cooed and kissed, and all manner of other verbs by all manner of other people. What's more, Ginny's students at Virginia Tech adore Sam in that endearing way of young adults who embrace wholeheartedly what they might one day have in their own lives. Once again, our son was passed around, from person-to-person. True, some of those people may well have been sick, but I now realize healthy communities of faith often treat babies in this manner. Brian Blount told me that his firstborn son was called "air baby" because, once he got to church, his feet never touched the ground!

In Sam's case, I must admit that he handled this attention very well; in fact, he seemed to love human contact, even to the point of leaning in and giving complete strangers his special, patented, *open*-mouthed kiss! I am aware that the ancient Christians used to greet one another with a kiss of peace; but Sam did not learn this practice by watching me. Talk about spreading germs! Yet Sam was obviously unconcerned . . . until, suddenly, something changed.

At about eight and a half months, this extroverted, saliva-swapping little person suddenly became, in the words of his mom, "a little cautious." Technically speaking, Sam developed what is known as "stranger anxiety." He used to be quite content while passed around any gathering of family or strangers. Almost overnight, the experience of finding himself in a new person's arms began to upset him. He would look around wildly for Ginny or me and, failing to see us, start to sob inconsolably until we held him again. I worried that he had picked up the anxiety gene from his dad.

My mother, as we've already seen, doubles as our family's expert on early childhood development; and so, she informed us that his newfound state of apprehension and unease was actually a natural, even beneficial, part of growing up. Upon realizing the absence of a trusted care-provider, children become upset, not only because they "miss" them, but on some level they correlate survival with those people's presence. What is overly sappy in a love song is downright true for a child: I need you to live.

After this stranger anxiety first manifested itself in his behavior, Sam developed this very specific look when he met a person for the first time. He'd train those big, baby blues on the new face, as if drinking down the image with his eyes. Then he'd raise an eyebrow as if to inquirer, *Can I trust you?* If I was holding him, I would "answer" by whispering reassuringly in his ear, "Yes, my love; you *can* trust this person."

It strikes me that the Parable of the Great Banquet challenges adults to work beyond our maladjusted form of stranger's anxiety, more typically defined as *prejudice.* Somewhere along life's way, many of us are taught to put up walls between "us" and "them." Yet, if we allow ourselves to get close enough, we can learn a great deal from people outside our race or class or worldview. Instead of economic and social systems based upon separateness and division, we can build communities of love, perhaps not with open-mouthed kisses, but fellowships that embody childlike joy just the same. By opening ourselves to others, we fully embrace God's gracious invitation. I contend that exhibiting such trust would be just as counter-cultural as the parable's guest list to the banquet, and likewise just as subversive of prejudices that still exist in our world. As difficult as it can be, I believe this is one of the defining characteristics of the strongest faith: to hear God's Spirit whispering, *Yes, my beloved; you can trust this person.*

For Sam's first birthday party, we made our own guest list that was mostly comprised of extended family and long-time friends. However, we also invited Sam's current caregiver and her boyfriend. We had known them for less time than any other person at the party, but their inclusion seemed perfectly natural. Sam loves them and so do we.

But, when Ginny extended the invitation in person, she asked tentatively, "Will it be alright with your family that my boyfriend is black?"

My heart breaks for our society today that anyone would still have to ask such a question. As I pray for a world without such divisions, I am grateful for the Parable of the Great Banquet's challenge that a strong faith is only as healthy as a loving community.

Priceless

The Parable of Talents or Pounds

In the ancient world, "talent" was purely an economic term that referred to a large measurement of silver. This definition is crystal clear from Matthew's Gospel (Mt 25:18). But I have heard many sermons on the famous Parable of the Talents that have spiritualized this word; indeed, the text seems to readily lend itself to an interpretation along the lines of, "Don't be afraid to make the most from what you have been given!"

I think this a good message for a father to impart to his son, albeit with some caveats in mind. For instance, I don't want Sam to feel pressure to follow in my footsteps. He doesn't have to love baseball or be a pastor or write books. In both sports and academics, I have witnessed the damaging impact that even well-intentioned parents can have upon their children. When I pray about his future, I truly want Sam to be himself; but I'd like for him to be his *best* self. Is this the message of the parable? More poignantly, is this the *only* message?

In previous chapters, we have observed how slight changes to the same parable can result in multiple interpretations. However, in this case, Luke's re-telling is *dramatically* unlike Matthew's version. By studying each version side-by-side, I hope to make the case that we can draw insight into our modern lives by balancing one narrative with the other. In so doing, we can avoid the pitfalls of misguided interpretations and perhaps take a step closer to becoming our best selves.

The Parable

Matthew 25:14–30	Luke 19:11–27
"For it is as if a person, before going away, summoned his own slaves and handed over his possessions to them. To one, he gave five talents; and to one, two; and to one, one, each according to his own ability; and then, he went away. Immediately the one who received five talents went and worked with them, and he earned five more. In the same way, the one with two earned two more. But the one who received one went off, dug up the soil, and hid his lord's silver. After a long period of time, the lord of those slaves came and settled accounts with them. The one who received five talents came forward and offered five more talents, saying: 'Lord, you handed over five talents to me. Look! I earned five more talents!' His lord replied to him, 'Excellent, noble and faithful slave; you were faithful over a few things, I will put you in charge over many things. Enter into the joy of your lord!' And the one with two talents came forward and said, 'Lord, you handed over two talents to me. Look! I earned two more talents!' His lord replied to him, 'Excellent, noble and faithful slave; you were	As they heard these things, he added a parable because he was near Jerusalem and they thought that the kingdom of God was going to appear immediately. Therefore he said, "A certain nobleman was going into a distant land to take royal power for himself and then return. After summoning ten of his own slaves, he gave ten pounds to them and said to them, 'Trade in these until I come.' But his citizens hated him and sent an embassy after him, saying: 'We do not want this one to rule over us.' When he returned after receiving royal power, he said to call those slaves to him to whom he had given the silver, in order that he might know what they gained by trading. So the first came near and said, 'Lord, your pound produced ten more pounds.' And he said to him, 'Well done, noble slave; because you were faithful in a lesser thing, have authority over ten cities!' And the second came and said, 'Your pound, Lord, made five pounds.' And so he said to that one, 'And you, be over five cities!' And another came and said, 'Lord, here is your pound, which I have stored away in a cloth,

faithful over a few things, I will put you in charge over many things. Enter into the joy of your lord!' And then the one who had received one talent came forward and said, 'Lord, I know you; that you are a harsh person, harvesting where you did not sow, and gathering from where you did not scatter seed. And because I was afraid, I went off and hid your talent in the soil. Look! You have what is yours.' By way of answering, his lord said to him, 'Wicked and lazy slave, did you understand that I harvest where I did not sow and gather from where I did not scatter seed? Then, you should have deposited my silver with the money-lenders, so that after I returned, I would obtain what was mine with interest. Therefore take the talent from him and give to the one who has ten talents! For to all who have, it will be given and will be in abundance; but to the one who does not have, even what he has will be taken away from him. And throw out the worthless slave into the outer darkness; there will be weeping and grinding of teeth.'"	for I was frightened by you because you are an exacting person, taking up what you did not put down and harvesting what you did not sow.' He said to him, 'I will judge you, wicked slave, from the words out of your mouth. Did you understand that I am an exacting man who takes up what I did not put down and harvests what I did not sow? Why then did you not give my silver to the money-lender? Then when I came, I might have collected it with interest.' And to the ones standing by, he said, 'Take the pound from him and give to the one who has ten pounds!' (But they said to him, 'Lord, he has ten pounds!') 'For I say to you that to all who have, it will be given; and from the one who does not have, even what he has will be taken away. Nevertheless bring my enemies here, the ones who did not want me to rule over them, and slaughter them before me!'"

Matthew

I realize that, if you've just read both versions, you most likely have more questions right now about the text in Luke! However, let's begin by studying Matthew's more familiar version, which is perhaps easier to comprehend (Mt 25:14–30). To summarize, a certain person goes on a long journey and, before he leaves, summons three slaves in order to give them a large and expensive measure of silver (talent) according to each one's ability. Two of them double their allotment, while the third buries his in the ground. Their lord returns, praises the two for their productivity and offers them a reward; then upbraids the third for his sloth and indolence before meting out his punishment. Seems relatively straightforward, doesn't it?

Well, as we have demonstrated with previous parables, redaction criticism often discovers meaning from the parable's placement in the larger narrative. Matthew the editor has placed the Parable of the Talents smack dab in the middle of his apocalyptic discourse, sandwiched between the Parable of the Ten Virgins (Mt 25:1–13) and the judgment of the nations (Mt 25:31–46). Especially in light of the themes found in the surrounding material, the majority of scholars understand this version of the parable as an allegory, meaning that each fictional component represents something else in the real world.[1] Accordingly, the lord's return to settle his accounts with his servants is a reference to the coming of the Son of Man and the Day of Judgment for all humankind.

Although this interpretation may appear to be direct and frank, this lord does seem very "harsh" when ordering the third slave thrown into the outer darkness with weeping and grinding of teeth (Mt 25:30). Such uncompromising severity does *not* match my understanding of God's grace and forgiveness; yet I recognize that the portrayal has a rhetorical effect. Matthew includes a clever play on words in which the third slave claims "to know" his lord, but his judgment is the result of the fact that he did not "understand" (Mt 25:24, 26). Through this analogy, God is depicted as such a strict taskmaster so that, while they have the chance, Matthew's readers would take to heart an urgent desire to multiply their God given "talents." This juxtaposition between "knowing" and "understanding" is the difference between

1. Dowling, *Taking Away the Pound*, 73

claiming to be "saved" and contemplating, "What am I saved *for*?" The punishment for the third slave's failure to act certainly drives home the point that Jesus emphasized earlier in this Gospel: don't hide your light under a bushel basket (Mt 5:15).

This parable asserts that the gift of God requires a faithful response. I also believe, however, that such exacting accountability needs to be balanced by biblical passages that emphasize other characteristics of God; for instance, the assertion that "nothing can separate us from the love of God" (Ro 8:38–39).

And now, let's think about this strange passage in Luke!

Luke

Initially one notices that the amount of money is measured in "pounds" rather than "talents." But that's not that big of a deal is it? Before we consider this and more dramatic differences, I want to point out the placement of this version in Luke's Gospel.

While Matthew has the Parable of the Talents as part of Jesus' teaching during his final days in Jerusalem, Luke records the Parable of the Pounds immediately *before* Jesus arrives in the Holy City (Luke 19:11). I have included verse eleven in my translation above because it flashes like a neon sign, telling readers that the following parable is used in a fundamentally different way than the apocalyptic text in Matthew. Indeed, Luke's rationale for telling this parable is that the disciples thought the kingdom of God was going to appear *immediately*. Obviously, they were not correct in this belief; and so, part of Luke's job as editor is to provide an alternative vision of the future.

If we look for clues about Luke's intention in the preceding narrative, we find descriptions of interactions between Jesus and various people that are decidedly about *this* world at *this* time. First, Jesus is unable to convince a rich ruler to distribute his wealth to the poor (18:18–30). Then Jesus heals a poor, blind beggar who becomes one of his followers (18:35–43). Finally we read the famous story of Zacchaeus, the "wee little man" who was also a very rich tax collector and gave half is money to the poor (19:8). The cast of characters is different, but the stories share themes about money and, more importantly, the just and equitable redistribution of that wealth.[2] While the allegorical interpretation made sense in light of Matthew's theology about the return of the Son of Man, it appears that Luke has an entirely different agenda in mind, which has far less to do with the afterlife than with how we use our resources on this side of eternity. How then do the various changes in the Parable of the Pounds reflect this purpose?

John Dominic Crossan has argued persuasively that Luke has combined *two* parables into one text. In addition to the Parable of the Pound, he identifies the other story as the Parable of the Throne-claimant.[3] Let me show you how he reached this conclusion by temporarily removing the verses that closely resemble Matthew's version. The remaining verses would read like this: a nobleman travels to obtain a kingdom (Luke 19:12); the citizens oppose his rule (19:14); despite that, the nobleman assumes power as their king (19:15); then even more people protest (19:25); because of their lack of support, the opponents of the king are slaughtered (19:27). In reading the text by separating the strands that Luke has woven together, the presence of

2. Dowling, 75–76

3. Crossan, *In Parables*, 94

a completely different parable is quite striking . . . and also extremely disturbing!

In the spring of 2010, I participated in a Bible study about Luke's text with a group of students from the Presbyterian campus ministry at the University of Virginia. Their eyes grew wide when I showed them the other parable twisted together with Matthew's more familiar version. Then one of the students cried out, "But the king of the parable is an *awful* person! How can he represent the God who *loves* us?" Great question! My answer is that he does *not* represent God!

As the college student intuited, Luke's nobleman is not a metaphorical representation of God, but rather a decidedly real-life portrayal of a vicious oppressor. In her adroit study, *Taking Away the Pound*, Elizabeth V. Dowling convincingly proves this man does things that God just wouldn't do. First, the nobleman "was going into a distant land to *take* royal power for himself" (Luke 19:12, emphasis mine). In light of the context of the verse, the nuance of this Greek verb, take, includes the notion of grasping and wrenching something away by brute force.[4] I suppose one could make the case that the Almighty God could act in this manner; but then, at the end of the parable, this usurper of the throne "slaughters" his opponents (Luke 19:27). Elsewhere in scripture, this same verb is used when the subject is either a blood thirsty mob (Ezek 16:10), a band of pitiless shepherds (Zech 11:5), or an evil tyrant (2 Macc 5:12, 24).[5] By his ruthless taking and slaughtering, this nobleman sounds exactly like a brutal dictator, and I think that's exactly the picture that would have come to mind for Luke's audience. History teaches that they were extremely familiar with such a "nobleman."

4. Dowling, 81

5. Dowling, 83

The ancient historian, Josephus, tells us that a man named Archelaus went to Rome in 4 BCE in order to "take" a kingdom. It was customary for people with a great deal of money to receive positions of power from the Emperor. Archelaus went to Caesar Augustus to gain control of the territory that had been ruled by his father, Herod. This transfer of power between family members was also a common practice back then. But then the plot thickens:

Josephus also tells us that "an embassy" of fifty Jews arrived in Rome at the same time in order to protest Archelaus' rise to power. Just before he went to Rome with his request, Archelaus had "slaughtered" three thousand of his countrymen in the temple precinct. Unfortunately for the Jewish protesters, Archelaus prevailed over his opponents, became the ruler of Judea, and then "slaughtered" the rest of those who were against him.[6] The similarities with the parable are striking: the people of the parable tried by every means possible to prevent the rise to power of a cruel man, yet they were ultimately defeated. The wealth of a few trumped the social protest of many, which ended in a terrifying scene of mass execution.

However, it really doesn't matter whether or not Luke was familiar with Josephus' specific account because this story of power, corruption, and violence has been a part of history in every age. The key, I think, is the message Luke wants to convey. With this image of carnage in mind, Luke brings Jesus into Jerusalem to confront the wealthy rulers in power with ways that are the complete *opposite* of this vicious nobleman (Luke 19:28). Jesus models a nonviolent alternative by standing up to the systems of unjust power and greed. His death and resurrection make it clear that loving sacrifice, not brutal conquest, is the means to receiving life in its abundance. It is a comfort to believe that such

6. Dowling, 81–82

a person is one's savior; but Luke would not want us to lose sight of the *challenge* that is entailed by attempting to follow Jesus to Jerusalem, thereby becoming Christ-like ourselves.

Conclusion

Our reading of Matthew's version is unsurprising and straightforward. In light of the expectation of the end of the world, the Parable of the Talents is an allegorical mandate for ethical behavior. Do the right thing with what you have been given! Keeping in mind that the talents were given to the servants in the first place, our need to respond faithfully to such God-given grace is clearly underlined. In reflecting upon the gift of his children, Christian Wiman describes sharing "the love that first led us out of ourselves and to each other."[7] It seems to me this beautiful and provocative description of love suggests something of what Matthew envisioned as a multiplication of talent.

Luke's Parable of the Pounds, however, is "devastating." This is the word John Dominic Crossan uses to describe a parable that is provocative in a decidedly disturbing manner. A devastating parable calls for nothing less than the complete reversal of our expectations.[8] For all the obvious differences across time and space, the modern Western world has sometimes looked an awful lot like the Roman Empire. This parable can be co-opted to support imperialism, free market economics, and manifest destiny. Jesus is believed to have blessed our way of life, even at the expense of others. Thanks be to God, then, that a close reading of Luke's parable offers a "devastating" alternative. We do not have to think of God as on the side of the oppressors nor do

7. Wiman, *My Bright Abyss*, 147

8. Crossan, 101–102

we have to teach this theology to our children. We can seek an alternative way of exercising power and using wealth, which is modeled on the life and teachings of Jesus.

Taken together, these two parables challenge us in terms of our individual behavior, yet also call into question the practices of economic and social exploitation. Ethical behavior is more complicated than simply earning a maximum profit by climbing the ladder, especially crushing others under one's heel to get to the top. No matter how many material resources we have acquired, we are called to assess the relationship between what we have been given and how we have been acting.

Alongside My Son

Waves of Fear

For a period of time shortly after his birth, Sam seemed to be trying to get *back* into the womb! I've read that the first three months of life are sometimes called the "fourth trimester" for this very reason. Whether held in someone's arms or gently placed in his bassinet, he would scrunch into a ball with his legs curled up and arms pressed to either side of his face. Ginny often put him into a type of sling that comfortably allowed him to naturally assume the fetal position. He *loved* this and often fell asleep immediately.

Who could blame the little guy for wanting to go back? First of all, he was much more familiar with that environment and, secondly, it seems much safer. You have that wondrous amniotic fluid to cushion you, surround you, and muffle loud noises. And think about this: food is pumped directly to you. No effort on your part at all! Sure, there's not much room in there; but then again, wide open spaces can be scary. It's a big world out here, full of uncertainty, full of anxiety. There are times when *in utero* seems like floating in your own personal sea of blessed calmness and holy serenity.

Speaking of oceans, Sam went to the beach for the first time when he was a little more than eight months. When he first gazed upon the *big* sea, his mouth literally dropped open in amazement! That is a priceless memory! Holding him in my arms that day, I tried to imagine what it must be like to glimpse the vastness of the Atlantic Ocean for the first time. He had no context for what lay before him, no way of anticipating or wrapping his mind around such an experience. I thought Sam was remarkably calm, his countenance much more serene than the choppy ocean about ten feet away.

Serene, that is, until I set him down on his own feet and the waves rushed around his ankles! Mind you, I had a firm grip around his little waist; but he still began to cry, actually trembling with fear! Maybe it was the relatively cold temperature of the salt water; or, perhaps the sensation that the ground was moving underneath him with the receding tide. The bottom line was that he was afraid.

For all the differences between the versions, both Matthew and Luke have the third slave justifying his actions because of *fear* (Mt 25:25; Luke 19:21). While things certainly do not end well for this trembling fellow, I appreciate his honesty. Often when adults, like me, are scared, we desire to hunker down somewhere we perceive as safe. I can easily recall times when, rather than allowing love to lead me out of myself and towards others, I have buried and stored away my gifts, both material and spiritual. Perhaps you can relate. The parable teaches, however, that "I was afraid" is not an acceptable excuse. It seems that the opposite of faith is fear, not doubt.

So I've come to believe that, for all the advantages and privileges we can offer Sam, one of the most important gifts is freedom. Specifically Ginny and I need to give him the freedom to *fear*. By no means am I referring to putting the "fear of God" in him. I never want him to be afraid of me. Nonetheless I do think it's important to allow him to wade into the water, experience new activities and situations, and thereby come into contact with awesome powers greater than him. As was true on his first day on the beach, this is not always pleasant. But you hope and pray that, with time and experience, the fear recedes like a wave back into your consciousness. In the future, I hope that Sam won't be afraid to get his feet wet. There is joy to be discovered while playing in the sparkling surf.

Pound of Gratitude

William R. Herzog describes a clergyman who taught the Parable of the Pounds to a group of peasants in Solentiname, Nicaragua at the height of that country's brutal dictatorship. Though this minister tried to inculcate the peasants with an allegorical interpretation more like Matthew's version, they argued that the parable described a cruel tyrant, *not* God.[9] These men and women had little formal education but were intimately familiar with what African scholar, Muse Dube, describes as "control at a distance" meaning the heavy-handed methods a few people of the ruling class use to extract wealth from the larger population.[10] People who have suffered through this exploitation and domination know in their heart of hearts that such abuse does not reflect the kingdom of God on earth. They are like the pro-

9. Herzog II, *Parables as Subversive Speech*, 155

10. Dube, "Toward A Post-Colonial Feminist Interpretation," 15

testers who decry the injustice of taking from the have-nots and giving to the haves (Luke 19:25).

And so, Luke's version of the parable prompts yet another hope for my son. I'd like to give him the opportunity to travel to other countries and visit with people from different cultures. I want him to see the world through different eyes, so he can learn to understand his life and his faith from other perspectives. For, though very cute and clever for his age, my dear son has done nothing to "earn" so many of the advantages he enjoys. He can't dress himself, but has more clothes than the majority of people in the world. He doesn't make any money, but his dad has accidentally lost enough change in his crib to constitute more than some hard-working people make in an entire day. His mom reads to him before tucking him into his crib, which means he will not be among the millions of people in his own country who are illiterate or homeless. These are the facts. What does a white, middle-class, American boy do with such knowledge?

It is one thing to be a baby gazing in wonder at the sea for the first time. Adults, however, need to have an appreciation of the larger context. We must try to understand the world around us, as enormous as it is, and the effects of a globalized economy, as complicated as it continues to be.

In light of these difficult tasks, I'm thankful that Luke uses the term, pounds, because there is a tendency in our Christian culture to over-spiritualize the word, talents, and thereby forget the concrete economic challenges of the Gospel. Preceding the Parable of the Pounds, Jesus instructs a rich ruler to sell everything and then laments that it is easier for a camel to pass through the eye of a needle than for a wealthy person to enter the kingdom of God (Luke 18:22–24). Sounds very *worldly* to me! But there are those who attempt to take the sting out of these sayings by making them metaphorical or figurative. Might such interpreters bury their heads in the sand and refuse to wrestle with the serious responsibility that comes with privilege?

I hasten to add that, just as fear can be crippling, so can guilt. I don't think it is constructive to shame anyone, even for a noble cause. Think about the oft quoted line from parents to their children at the dinner table: "Clean your plate! There are other children starving in the world." That's just not helpful; hungry children are not assisted by your upset stomach! Instead, Luke's intertwining of these two parables makes it clear that we must blend personal accountability with the cultivation of an awareness of injustices. Allow me to unpack that statement:

Gazing at the world through the lens of my class, gender, and culture, I was much more likely to interpret either version of this parable as a call to hard work and individual achievement. Based on my upbringing and experience, it was easy for me to spiritualize the meaning of the word, talent. Other people bring different perspectives to the task of interpretation, which does not necessarily mean my initial interpretation was "wrong." It means that I have the *mandate* to learn from those who have lived through the different experiences, such as the peasants in Nicaragua or the theologian in Africa. As a result of this knowledge, I may be called to repentance, perhaps in terms of how I spent my money or turned a blind eye to my country's tacit support of an authoritarian regime.

But gratitude is a better teacher than guilt. If you like, please use my blessing for Sam with your own children or for yourself: freed from guilt, may he serve freely; blessed with resources to share, may he open his heart to what others can give.

Like it or not, Sam will never be able to get back into the womb. As he grows up, I want to give my child many "talents." I want to provide for his needs and, truthfully, grant many of his desires as well, even if a few are rather frivolous in the long term. And I will also work to share a larger worldview with him, so that he might come to terms with what he has received. I hope that he will do something more with these gifts, prayerfully reaching out to others with an awareness of their needs. Though one could never put a price on such behavior, learning compassion is a multiplication of talent.

The Morning Light

The Parable of the Fig Tree

I used to be hesitant to tell the person sitting next to me on a plane or in a coffee shop what exactly I do for a living. Upon learning that you are a pastor, a complete stranger might take out years of frustration with organized religion on *you*!

It is almost as awkward when a believer launches into an opinion about the so-called "last days." People reference this tragic event or that cultural trend, and then claim that our lives are only going to get worse. They justify such predictions by saying, "Everything is happening just like the Bible says." When I hear this kind of rhetoric, part of me still wants to escape to another seat. However, I've come to appreciate the importance of thoughtfully and respectfully engaging others in the very types of conversations I used to avoid. It is ironic that, since I want to work for a better world in the days ahead, I must help to educate people about what the Gospels *actually* say about the end.

Just before the crucifixion, three Gospels record a parable in response to the disciples' request for a "sign" about the future (Mt 24:3; Mark 13:4; Luke 21:7). Such biblical texts that envision the "last days" are more formally known as "apocalyptic" literature. This word, apocalypse, does not mean "doomsday" but comes from the Greek word for "revelation." The disciples literally wanted Jesus to *reveal* the future. In this, they were very much like us. We would love to know what tomorrow holds; and so, are overly receptive to speculations about the "signs of the times" from preachers, writers, television shows, and movies. As a result, there is a heightened level of anxiety in our culture; and yet, many of these prognosticators claim to be followers of the same person known for teaching, "Do not be anxious" (Mt 6:25–34). How do we account for this contradiction? It turns out there is something missing . . .

In the New Testament, the Greek word for "anxiety" is composed of the prefix for "part of" and the verb that means "to remember." Anxiety, then, is literally defined as remembering only in part, such as one portion of the larger narrative or focusing exclusively on the negative aspect. As an antidote, we need to teach people about the *whole* story.

With that motivation in mind, let's learn from the fig tree so that we might discover a complete message of faith for our children's future.

The Parable

Mark 13:28–29	Matthew 24:32–33	Luke 21:29–31
"Learn the parable from the fig tree: when its branch has already become tender and is putting forth leaves, then you know that summer is near. So also, when you see these things occurring, you know that he is near, at the doors."	"Learn the parable from the fig tree: when its branch has already become tender and is putting forth leaves, then you know that summer is near. So also, when you see all these things, you know that he is near, at the doors."	And he told a parable to them, "See the fig tree and all the trees! When they have already sprouted, you can look for yourselves and know that summer is already near. So also, when you see these things occurring, you know that the kingdom of God is near."

Mark

As students of the New Testament, it is hugely relevant to note that this parable is the *only* time in his entire Gospel that Mark uses the verb, "to learn." It is as if he says, "Let the fig tree become your teacher."[1] So our lesson is gleaned from careful observation of the natural world. Like contemplating the natural area around a grove of trees, this very short parable is understood by studious consideration of its surrounding verses. Just before this teaching, we read a stark warning from Jesus: "Many will come in my name and say, 'I am he!' and they will lead many astray . . . When you hear of wars and rumors of wars, do not be alarmed" (Mark 13:6–7). Clearly, this instruction stands in sharp contrast to the doomsday prophecies that attempt to frighten people. If we are to learn from the fig tree as it cycles through the natural seasons of growth, then we must first slow down and remain calm. A refreshing thought, yes?

This "first-take-a-deep-breath" approach is further developed by the inclusion of another parable that has been identified as a "parable of balance" (Mark 13:34–37).[2] If you remember our last chapter, the beginning should sound familiar: it echoes the parables about "talents" and "pounds" in which a man goes away on a journey and leaves his servants in charge (Mt 25:14–15; Luke 19:12–13). But by the end of this shorter passage, Mark would have us learn a different lesson: stay awake (Mark 13:37). Ched Myers has noted the irony that this is the exact instruction the disciples were unable to obey in the Garden of Gethsemane (Mark 14:32–41).[3] Our challenge, then, is not only to stay calm, but also to remain alert.

1. Nolland, *The Gospel of Matthew*, 987
2. Donahue and Harrington, *The Gospel of Mark*, 377
3. Myers, *Binding the Strong Man*, 347

If we continue to contemplate these two parables together, I think our lesson becomes even clearer. In Mark's version, the master gives neither talents nor pounds, but "authority" to his slaves (Mark 13:34). While "learn" is a key word in the Parable of the Fig Tree because it is used only once, I believe "authority" is the term that illumines the meaning of this parable of balance, conversely because it is used on *multiple* occasions in the Gospel of Mark. This is the same word that Jesus uses to teach (Mark 1:22), forgive sins (Mark 2:10), and cast out demons (Mark 3:15). It was the same "authority" that he gave to the twelve disciples (Mark 6:7). At the conclusion of this other parable, Jesus extends that authoritative power: "What I say to you, I say to *all*" (Mark 13:37). Therefore, rather than believing the current generation is doomed, Jesus has given us the authority to make the world better!

In summary, the two parables strike a perfect balance–a duet of patience and action. While watching the growth of leaves is a metaphor for waiting for God to enter decisively into human history, we are commanded to use our God-given authority. In Mark's skillful narrative, we learn a valuable lesson: true discipleship consists, not of fearful speculation concerning a gloomy future, but of deeply focused attention to the present moment in order to make a positive difference.

But Matthew and Luke do not include this second parable. What lesson might they teach us?

Matthew and Luke

In the previous chapter, we have studied the different ways in which Matthew and Luke expanded the much smaller version of the other "parable of balance" found in Mark 13:34–37. Yet only Luke makes significant changes to the

Parable of the Fig Tree. Let's first examine how Matthew seems to echo Mark's theology, before asserting Luke's distinctive emphasis.

At the risk of putting my readers to sleep, I have to lapse into a little "grammar-speak" in order to draw a conclusion from Matthew's parable. (Perhaps this is a good opportunity for you to practice focused concentration!) The linking verb found in the final clause of both versions lacks a personal pronoun (Mt 24:32; Mark 13:29). This minor detail proves highly significant because Greek verbs in the third person singular do not identify the specific gender of their subjects. It is clear that Jesus likened the growth of fig leaves to the coming of summer, but grammatically speaking, the next phrase could read "*she–he–it* is the near the gates." Therefore it is left up to the interpreter to make this choice. How exciting!

I'm not quite sure who "she" would be in this apocalyptic scenario, but "it" could refer to a phenomenon like the end of the world or the end of time.[4] However, most scholars believe that "he" is the better translation because both Mark and Matthew intended to refer to the coming Son of Man.[5] But if the verb could refer to either subject, then the editors closely connected the end of time (it) with the return of Jesus (he). Since the comparison regards the fig tree and the relatively quick arrival of summer after the leaves appear on its branches, this meant that the end was thought to be very soon and, therefore, Mark and Matthew assumed they were writing in the last days. Note that Jesus is reported as claiming unambiguously that the current generation will live to see "all these things" take place (Mt 24:34; Mark 13:30).

4. Nolland, 988

5. Donahue and Harrington, 375

Now, here's the part that is even more exciting: Luke *substitutes* "the kingdom of God" as the subject of the second clause! Not only does this absolve the ambiguity of Mark's version, this simple edit fundamentally alters the meaning.[6] Luke Timothy Johnson contends that, contrary to both Mark and Matthew, Luke was trying to generalize the final judgment to a non-specific time.[7] Support for this claim is drawn from surrounding material. For instance, Luke tells us to resist the temptations of *daily* life (Luke 21:34) and keep awake in *every* season (Luke 21:36). In his version of our parable, he even adds "all the trees" to the reference to the fig tree, as if he didn't want to get too specific (Luke 21:29).[8] These changes give the overall impression that Luke was *not* counting on Jesus to return any time soon.

I think such observations naturally lend themselves to thinking about the original audience of the Gospels, particularly because Matthew and Luke wrote after Mark. In terms of the their *eschatology* (meaning the study of the last days), Eric Franklin identifies the dilemma faced by both Matthew and Luke as editors: "[Both] are caught up in the problem of relating eschatology and history . . . both have to come to terms with the fact that history has gone on . . . both have to respond to the situation brought about by the passing of time and by the continuing hiddenness of the reign of God."[9] Matthew and Luke had to instill a sense of purpose to those followers of Jesus who were still waiting for his return. Like Mark, this undoubtedly included the notion of staying alert and attending to the important work at hand. Yet as more and more time passed, these editors

6. Johnson, *The Gospel of Luke*, 328

7. Johnson, 330

8. Johnson, 328

9. Franklin, *Luke*, 166

also had to keep hope alive. Without proper motivation, one can only "stay awake" for so long!

Through our study of the parables, we find evidence of a significant difference between Matthew and Luke regarding the coming kingdom. With our analysis of both the Parable of the Great Banquet and the Parable of the Talents, we concluded that Matthew edited that material to exhort his audience to ethical behavior in light of an imminent judgment. This chapter's parable further emphasizes this motivation: we learn from the fig tree that we should watch for the Son of Man to come and usher in this kingdom in the near future, as quickly as summer follows spring. To be clear, I don't think Luke would disagree completely with this theology.

But, again referring to the earlier parables, we observed that Luke's versions were decidedly more about creating a just world on this side of eternity. Furthermore, in a passage that Leo Tolstoy made famous, Luke describes the kingdom of God as "within you" (Luke 17:21). This phrase could also be translated as "among you," but the overarching idea is that the kingdom is *already* present.[10] His slight alterations to the Parable of the Fig Tree likewise imply that we can experience that kingdom right here, right now.

Conclusion

Donald McKim refers to the "eschatological itch" as the overwhelming desire to share personal opinions about the last days and, consequently, make such speculations the centerpiece of one's theology.[11] In reference to this itch, I have suggested that obsessive "scratching" leads to anxiety

10. Franklin, 268

11. McKim, *Presbyterian Questions, Presbyterian Answers*, 97

because it focuses too exclusively on a single aspect of a much bigger story of God and human history. Blessed relief comes by remembering the big picture: at some glorious moment in time, God is going to make things right in the world.

A desire for ultimate divine redemption motivated the disciples to ask Jesus for a sign long ago. Years later, the communities addressed by the Gospels were certainly asking the same questions. And so, the Parable of the Fig Tree was edited skillfully in order to give hope with the passing of each season, such as from spring to summer and from childhood to parenthood. In classic theological terms, this paradox between the future and the present is known as "already and not yet."[12] This implies the spiritual balm for the eschatological itch is also a challenge: we have a responsibility to live our faith today.

Alongside My Son

An Ultrasound Apocalyptic

Particularly in our technological age, when news from across the world is instantly available with the touch of a button, there will always be grist for end-of-time predictions. In the few weeks after Sam was born, a "superstorm" known as Sandy decimated much of New England; then Israel attacked Hamas in the Gaza Strip for eight straight days. Since I was up at all hours of the night with a newborn, I had plenty of opportunities to follow these stories. Indeed I was amazed at the up-to-the-minute, breaking

12. For those interested, I have written more about eschatology and apocalyptic theology in my book, *Take My Hand: A Theological Memoir.* See especially chapter 11, "Come, Lord Jesus!"

news coverage that is available even at three o'clock in the morning. Some would argue this is not a good thing.

But our modern world also has indisputable technological advantages. For example, the machine called a 3D-ultrasound is utterly amazing. Months before Sam was born, we actually saw the features of his face! His image was projected onto a screen and we experienced his presence, as he waved his little arms and kicked his tiny feet–we even saw him swallow amniotic fluid. And yet, we *still* had to wait for his birth. Like the church's teaching about the kingdom of God on earth, our baby was "already and not yet." It turns out that apocalyptic theology would overlap in other ways with our appointment.

Our ultrasound technician had a fondness for making chit-chat and asked what we did for a living. Ginny told him we were pastors, and this started a conversation about (you guessed it!) the "last days." He started talking about all the wars, famines, and earthquakes that Jesus said would occur before he came back to earth.

At first, I held my tongue. Truthfully I was far more interested in the images of my unborn child right in front of me than the technician's speculations about the Middle East. But this man was persistent! Even though I kept directing his attention back to the screen, he kept returning to his conspiracy theories. Finally, I gave in. I spoke in my best pastor tone-of-voice, "Here's the thing you should remember; instead of trying to predict the *end of time*, I believe we should have faith in God *at all times*." With that, I leaned back in my chair, rather proud of the parallel structure of my off-the-cuff remark. (I did notice, however, that Ginny rolled her eyes.)

"So," the technician replied, equally unimpressed, "Does that mean that you just don't ever think about the end-of-times? Are you saying that I shouldn't worry about living in the last days?"

"Well, you can think about it as much as you like; but just do so with trust in your heart." That didn't strike me as convincing enough, so I added, "You know, Jesus often said, 'Don't be anxious.'"

Then, wanting to squelch any follow-up questions, I changed the subject. "Do you have any children?"

Albeit with a lack of rhetorical sophistication, this proved to be my wisest comment. It turns out that he did have a son. He began describing him and his hobbies. As an afterthought, he mentioned that he had overseen all of the ultrasounds for his wife's pregnancy.

"Wow," I replied, now genuinely interested, "What was that like?"

"Well, you have to understand that I know all the *signs* to look for. When things got a little dicey late in her pregnancy, we went straight to the emergency room for a C-section."

He paused and the whole room became very still.

"Before something awful happened, we went in and *got* my son."

On that day, it was the ultrasound technician (not the pastors in the room) who offered the profound insight into the apocalypse. What if we thought of God as watching the signs of the times in order to *rescue* us? So assured, we could focus our full attention on helping and taking care of one another. As I've studied the Parable of the Fig Tree, I've been grateful for this conversation that I didn't want to have and a teacher I didn't expect to be revealed.

Anxiety Antidote

The Gospels exhort us to stay awake, which is not a problem for those who take care of newborns!

While in graduate school, I became somewhat accustomed to long stretches of study without sleep; however, there is a unique patina of exhaustion on one's face after the arrival of a new baby. And that's when the mental confusion sets in. My mom's friend came home one evening shortly after his son was born and couldn't figure out why in the world his car's remote key wouldn't unlock the door . . . to his *house*! Your hope is that such delirium is only temporary.

But when Sam was about five-months-old, Ginny and I experienced the disorienting effects of sleep deprivation for a second time. Our baby boy reverted to his newborn habit of waking up every one to two hours. *Every one to two hours!* Then he would scream until one of his bleary-eyed parents trudged into the nursery and rocked him back to sleep. It was during this time that I learned a new form of prayer. After gently setting my sleeping child down in his crib, I'd tip-toe away fervently pleading to God that he would remain asleep; but if he woke up, please Lord let it be *Ginny* who hears him first!

Laying aside the possibility of divine intervention, it was true that my blessed wife was summoned by the screams more often; she alone could nurse the baby back to sleep. Even when Sam was quiet, she would lie awake in anticipation. You just never knew when the next round of tears would start, which must be something like Chinese water torture. After weeks of irregularly interrupted nights, she turned to me one bright morning with dark circles under her blue eyes and lamented, "I've had enough." What she meant is that she was ready to try a "sleep training" method.

Before Sam was born, I was told by various people that the best way to get a baby to stop crying and go to sleep was to lay him down in the crib, shut the door, and then take a shower until the hot water runs out. But we had decided that we would not let our child "cry it out." Our foremost concern was his safety: children communicate through crying. It is their way of telling caregivers that they need attention. We didn't want Sam to conclude that, when he was hurting or scared or upset, his parents wouldn't be there for him. Imagine how you would feel if no one acknowledged your cries for help. And so, we attempted a number of "no-cry sleep strategies" with varying degrees of success.[13] Yet, by seven months, we were literally at our wits end.

We introduced a variation of the famous Ferber method.[14] Instead of rocking him to sleep, we put Sam in the crib while still awake. He'd scream himself purple for exactly three minutes; then one of us would go back into the room. However (and this is the key), we did *not* hold him until he fell back to sleep. After offering some reassuring words in a soft voice about how much we loved him, we'd leave the room again. The method gradually increases the amount of time between visits (from five minutes to ten to fifteen and so on) until, eventually, the child stops fussing and falls asleep. Through the excruciating wait, I found that it helpful to pray for God's presence to be with our child.

It was also useful to learn that, despite our initial reservations, our baby was not being tortured. The basic procedure outlined above was developed through legitimate

13. I would recommend reading Elizabeth Pantley's book, *The No-Cry Sleep Solution: Gentle Ways to Help Your Baby Sleep Through the Night.*

14. Ferber, *Solve Your Child's Sleep Problems*

scientific study. Our natural sleep cycles only last about two to three hours for our entire lives; however, the majority of adults have learned to seamlessly connect these cycles without interruption, so that we don't wake up dazed and confused and screaming. Babies need to develop the ability to move in and out of sleep cycles on their own, and well-meaning parents can actually hinder this process. Don't misunderstand me: some of my happiest moments were spent snuggling my son as he drifted off to sleep. But, imagine if you fell asleep in the arms of your loved one, and then woke up in a different place with no idea how you got there or why you were alone. You'd probably scream yourself purple!

Therefore my understanding that Sam was learning to "self-soothe" was more reassuring than the science of sleep. While we wanted him to develop this skill on his own, there was a major way in which we could continue to help. When we commenced the sleep training regimen, we also introduced a "lovey." This refers to a soft object that Sam could hold whenever he went to sleep. (Incidentally, this is why the experts, including Dr. Ferber, recommend delaying this method until the child is at least six-months-old because there is little danger of suffocation via an object in the crib.) In this case, his lovey was a green blanket, lovingly knit for him by a special friend named Sally. To this day, Sam sleeps with this blanket. When we put him down either for a nap or for the night, he promptly stuffs his lovey in his mouth and soothes himself to sleep. This blanket is his antidote for anxiety; now he regularly sleeps through the night. Thanks be to God!

Let me conclude by offering some reassuring words as a pastor. When Jesus spoke of the last days, I don't think he wanted us to toss and turn through sleepless nights of anxious waiting for the apocalypse. Like a child learns to connect his or her sleep cycles, a mature faith is also self-soothing by trusting in God's care from beginning to end–a lovey of faith. We remember the whole story about God our Creator, Redeemer, and Sustainer; our God who declares that creation is good (Gen 1), promises never to abandon us (John 14:18), and gives us a peace that passes all understanding (Phil 4:7). You might mention this theology to any loved ones suffering from an eschatological itch, perhaps even the next stranger who engages you in conversation about the last days.

But admittedly, I have trouble practicing what I preach. As I've edited this book, I've noticed my "anxiety itch" crops up quite a bit. About as often as scripture advises us not to be anxious, *Parables of Parenthood* contains an example of my worried scratching! Perhaps this is part of the human condition. It is difficult to come to terms with the reality of an unknown future, which is especially anxiety-producing as a parent.

The Gospels, however, offer an antidote for anxiety, a spiritual relief for the itch: take a deep breath, trust God with the future, and focus on this present moment. Of course, I do not know what tomorrow will be like for my son, much less the rest of human history. The kingdom of God is already and not yet; as sure as the fig tree sprouts leaves, we are taught that a new kingdom will be revealed.

But that doesn't mean that I need to be afraid.

I can choose to live with the faith of a child who soothes himself through the night, trusting that the morning light will reveal his father standing at the door.

Afterword

Dear Sam,

I love to read books to you, my love. Your dad and I are so pleased that you seem to love it too! We have books stacked all over the house and for a long time you found great joy in throwing them off tables, one-by-one. You continue to enjoy doing this, but now when you throw books down, it is in search of the one you want us to read. When you see the one you want you stop, say "da," wave your arms, and look at us with a smile. This works every time! When I take the book in my hand and lift you onto my lap, you always let out the sweetest little chuckle that lets me know how excited you are to read together. I felt a lot like this while I was reading Dad's book. It is a gift to me, and I sincerely hope one day you will treasure it as well.

This book is a beautiful piece of art that shows us how the teachings of Jesus, especially his parables, connect us in ways so much deeper than words. It's kind of like your "touch and feel" books, which are some of your favorites right now. You take such delight in lifting flaps and touching different textures! I think that Dad's book is like adding flaps and textures to the Bible. The stories that he tells about us help other people to connect to the very old stories that Jesus tells. Our stories are actually part of God's story.

I believe that the Bible is God's living, breathing Word because the Holy Spirit helps us find ourselves in its pages. Your Dad makes this clear in his book when he weaves together the messages of Jesus with the lessons we are learning from you. Both Jesus and you are our teachers!

You have been teaching me, my dear one, since the day you were born. For over twelve hours, you and I worked gruelingly together to bring you out of my womb and into the outside world. There were moments I felt like I was not able to push you through. You gave me strength I didn't know I had; your heartbeat remained steady and healthy through the whole delivery. And, once you were safely resting on my chest, I've never felt stronger.

I've also never felt more vulnerable. I loved you so much that my heart felt like it was on the outside of my body. If anything bad happened to you, I felt I couldn't bear it. Yet I was aware that possibility was ultimately out of my control. As your dad wrote, such control is an illusion. But how could I feel so fierce and fragile at the same time?

This is what I know in my heart, even to this day; you have taught me that strength and vulnerability are inextricably linked. Jesus actually taught the same thing!

Your dad wrote a lot about what Jesus called "the kingdom of heaven." It comes up quite a bit in the parables when we are challenged to help bring about God's kingdom on earth, right now. One of the hardest parts about this is that Jesus teaches us that the kingdom of heaven often turns our world upside down. In God's kingdom, the weak are powerful, the last are first, and children are lifted up as leaders.

As you grow up, you will hear different messages from our society. Vulnerability is usually linked with weakness and is understood as something to avoid. Strength is seen as the superior opposite of vulnerability. If you are strong, you cannot be hurt. This is just not true, nor is it desirable.

To be vulnerable is, in truth, to be strong; opening yourself to love, to the other, to God, is the most powerful act of all. And you (and Jesus!) have taught me that lesson I will never forget.

I love to read books to you because I want you to learn from them, but also because I love to feel close to you. When we look at books together, you snuggle in my lap and I can smell your hair and feel your cheek close to mine. This brings me more joy than I can tell you. Likewise we read the parables of Jesus not only to learn from them, but also to feel close to God.

I hope that you, Dad, and me will always feel connected as we continue to live our story in the great lap of God.

Love,
Mom
November, 2013

Bibliography

Blount, Brian K., and Gary Charles, *Preaching Mark in Two Voices*. Louisville and London: Westminster John Knox Press, 2002.

Boring, M. Eugene. "The Gospel of Matthew: Introduction, Commentary, and Reflections." *The New Interpreter's Bible, Vol. 8*. Nashville: Abingdon Press, 1995.

Brueggemann, Walter. *Prayers for a Privileged People*. Nashville: Abingdon Press, 2008.

Carroll, John T. *Luke: A Commentary*. Louisville and London: Westminster John Knox Press, 2012.

Craddock, Fred. *Luke* (Interpretation: A Bible Commentary for Teaching and Preaching) Louisville, KY: John Knox Press, 1990.

Crossan, John Dominic. *The Historical Jesus: The Life of a Mediterranean Jewish Peasant*. New York: HarperCollins Publishers, 1991.

———. *In Parables: The Challenge of the Historical Jesus*. Sonoma, CA: Polebridge Press, 1992.

Culpepper, R. Alan. "The Gospel of Luke: Introduction, Commentary, and Reflections." *The New Interpreter's Bible, Vol. 9*. Nashville: Abingdon Press, 1995.

Danker, Frederick William. *A Greek-English Lexicon of the New Testament and other Early Christian Literature. 3rd Ed.* Chicago and London: University of Chicago Press, 2000.

Donahue, John R., and Daniel J. Harrington, *The Gospel of Mark* (Sacra Pagina). Collegeville, MN: Liturgical Press, 2002.

Dowling, Elizabeth V. *Taking Away the Pound: Women, Theology, and the Parable of the Pounds in the Gospel of Luke*. New York: T&T Clark International, 2007.

Dube, Musa W. "Toward A Post-Colonial Feminist Interpretation of the Bible." *Semeia* 78 (1997): 11–26.

Ehrman, Bart D. *The New Testament: A Historical Introduction to the Early Christian Writings. Third Edition.* (New York and Oxford: Oxford University Press, 2004).

Ferber, Richard. *Solve Your Child's Sleep Problems: New, Revised, and Expanded Edition.* New York: Fireside, 2006.

Franklin, Eric. *Luke: Journal for the Study of the New Testament Supplement* (Book 92). Sheffield: Sheffield, 1994.

Hare, Douglas R.A. *Matthew* (Interpretation: A Bible Commentary for Teaching and Preaching). Louisville, KY: John Knox Press, 1993.

Hauerwas, Stanley. *Matthew* (Brazos Theological Commentary on the Bible). Grand Rapids, MI: Brazos Press, 2006.

Herzog II, William R. *Parables as Subversive Speech: Jesus as Pedagogue of the Oppressed.* Louisville and London: Westminster John Knox Press, 1994.

Lischer, Richard. "The Sermon on the Mount as Radical Pastoral Care." *Interpretation* 41. 1987.

———. *Stations of the Heart: Parting with a Son.* New York: Alfred A. Knopf, 2013.

McKim, Donald. *Presbyterian Questions, Presbyterian Answers: Exploring Christian Faith.* Louisville: Geneva Press, 2003.

Myers, Ched. *Binding the Strong Man: A Political Reading of Mark's Story of Jesus.* Maryknoll, NY: Orbis Books, 1988.

Nolland, John. *The Gospel of Matthew* (The New International Greek Testament Commentary). Grand Rapids, MI: Wm. B. Eerdmans Publishing Co., 2005.

Norris, Kathleen. *Amazing Grace: A Vocabulary of Faith.* New York: Riverhead Books, 1998.

Pantley, Elizabeth. *The No-Cry Sleep Solution: Gentle Ways to Help Your Baby Sleep Through the Night.* New York: The McGraw-Hill Companies, 2002.

Perkins, Pheme."The Gospel of Mark: Introduction, Commentary, and Reflections." *The New Interpreter's Bible, Vol. 8.* Nashville: Abingdon Press, 1995.

Perrin, Norman. *Jesus and the Language of the Kingdom.* Minneapolis: Fortress Press, 1980.

Ringe, Sharon H. *Luke* (Westminster Bible Companion). Louisville and London: Westminster John Knox Press, 1995.

Rosenthal, Amy Krouse. *Plant a Kiss,* illus. by Peter H. Reynolds. Harper: New York, 2012.

Saint-Exupéry, Antoine. *The Little Prince.* Translated by Katherine Woods. Boston, MA: Harcourt Children's Books, 1971.

Senior, Donald S. *The Gospel of Matthew.* Nashville: Abingdon Press, 1997.

Stern, Frank. *A Rabbi Looks at Jesus' Parables.* Lanham, Boulder, New York, Toronto, Oxford: Rowman & Littlefield Publishers, Inc., 2006.

Tyson, Timothy B. *Blood Done Sign My Name: A True Story.* New York: Three Rivers Press, 2004.

Williamson, Lamar. *Mark* (Interpretation: A Bible Commentary for Teaching and Preaching). Louisville, KY: John Knox Press, 1983.

Wiman, Christian. *My Bright Abyss: Meditation of a Modern Believer.* New York: Farrar, Straus and Giroux, 2013.

Made in the USA
Columbia, SC
04 January 2019